Dark Light
Michael Martone
Lustrum Press

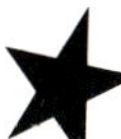

Printed by the Rapoport Printing Corp., New York
I.S.B.N. Number 0-912-810-11-4 (soft) 0-912-810-12-2 (hard)
Library of Congress Number 73-88291
Back cover photo: USA Censorship, June 21, 1973
For my Friends

It needed in the first instance
a bright light to expose
and a dark light to expose...

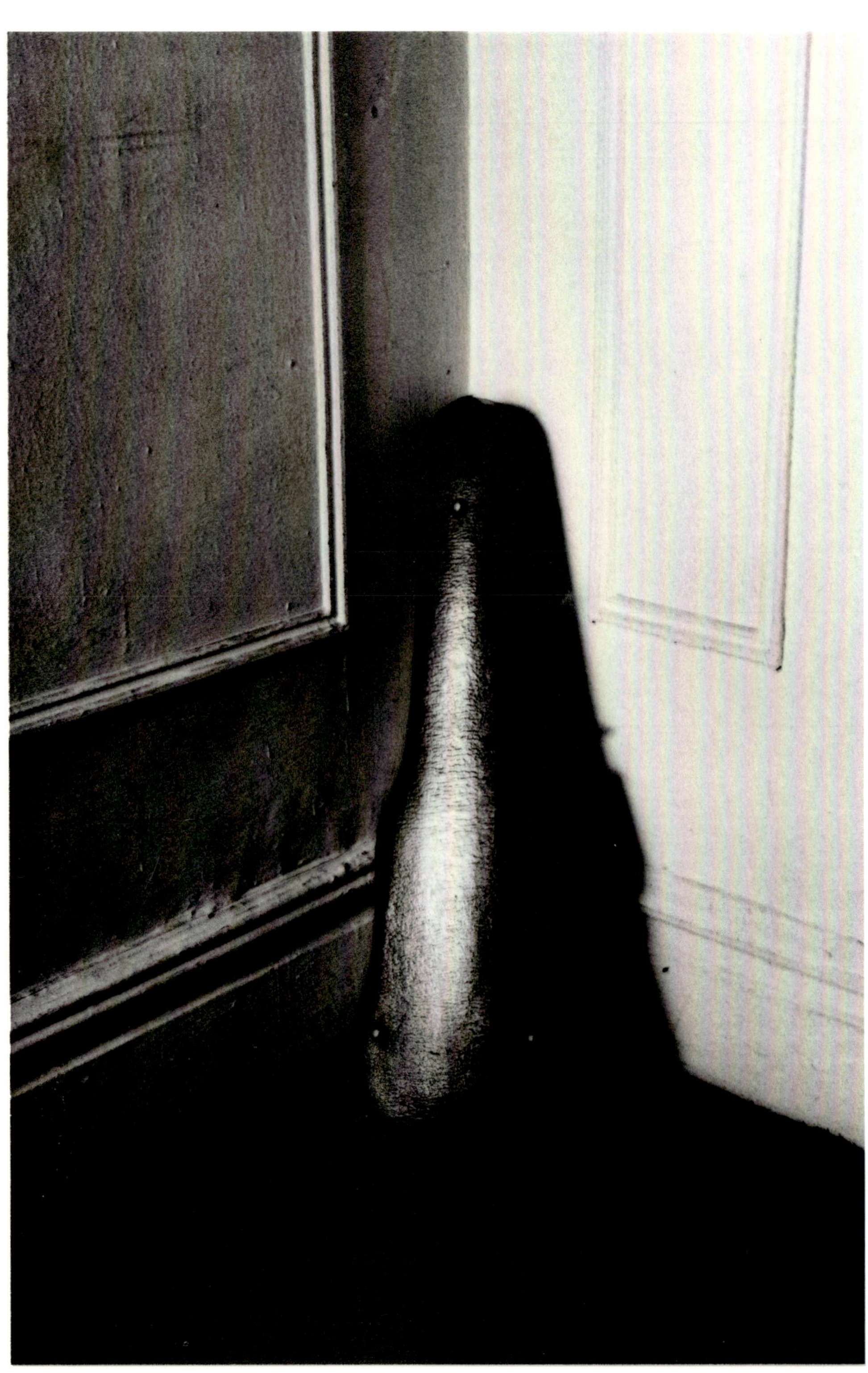

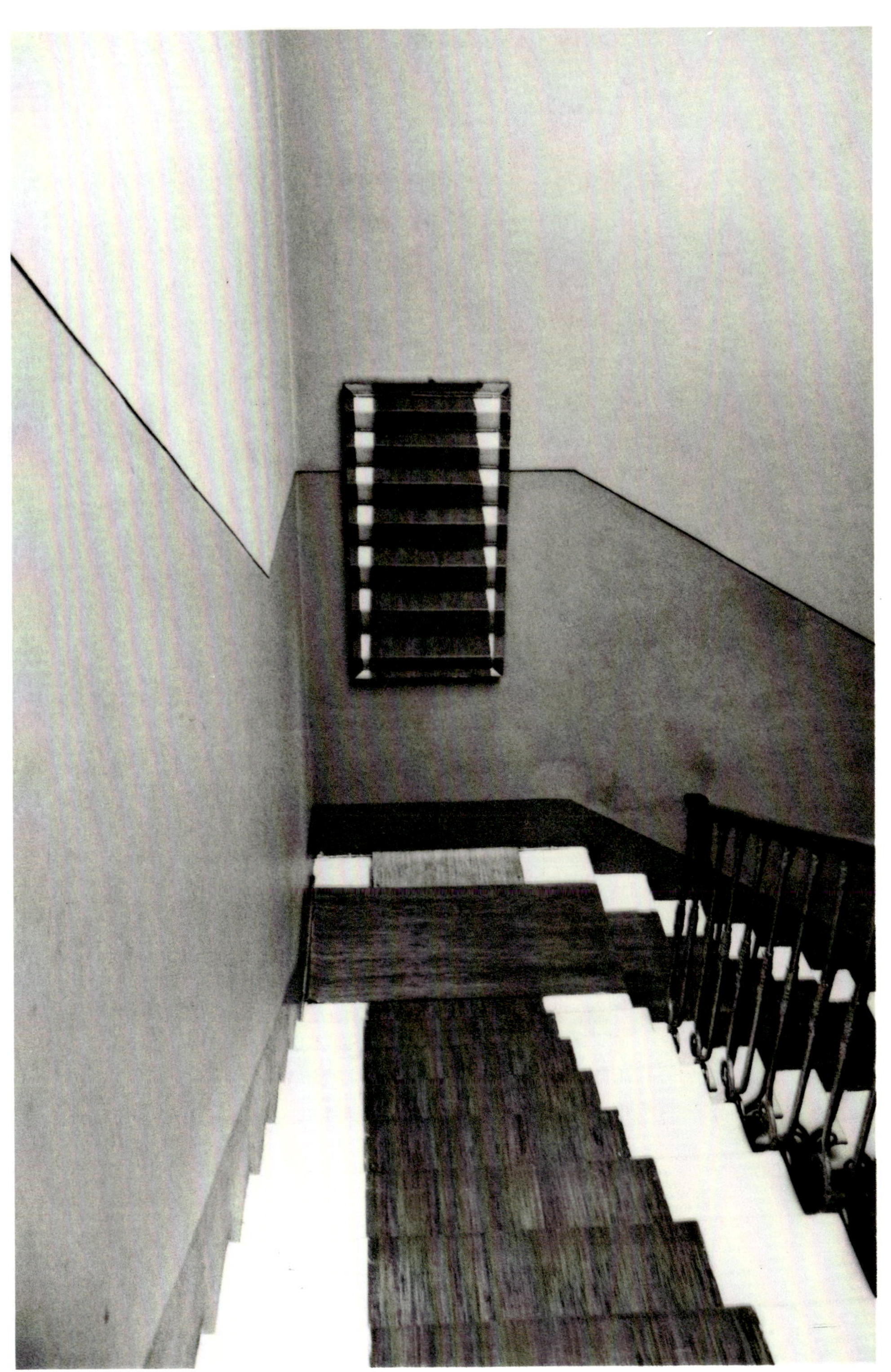

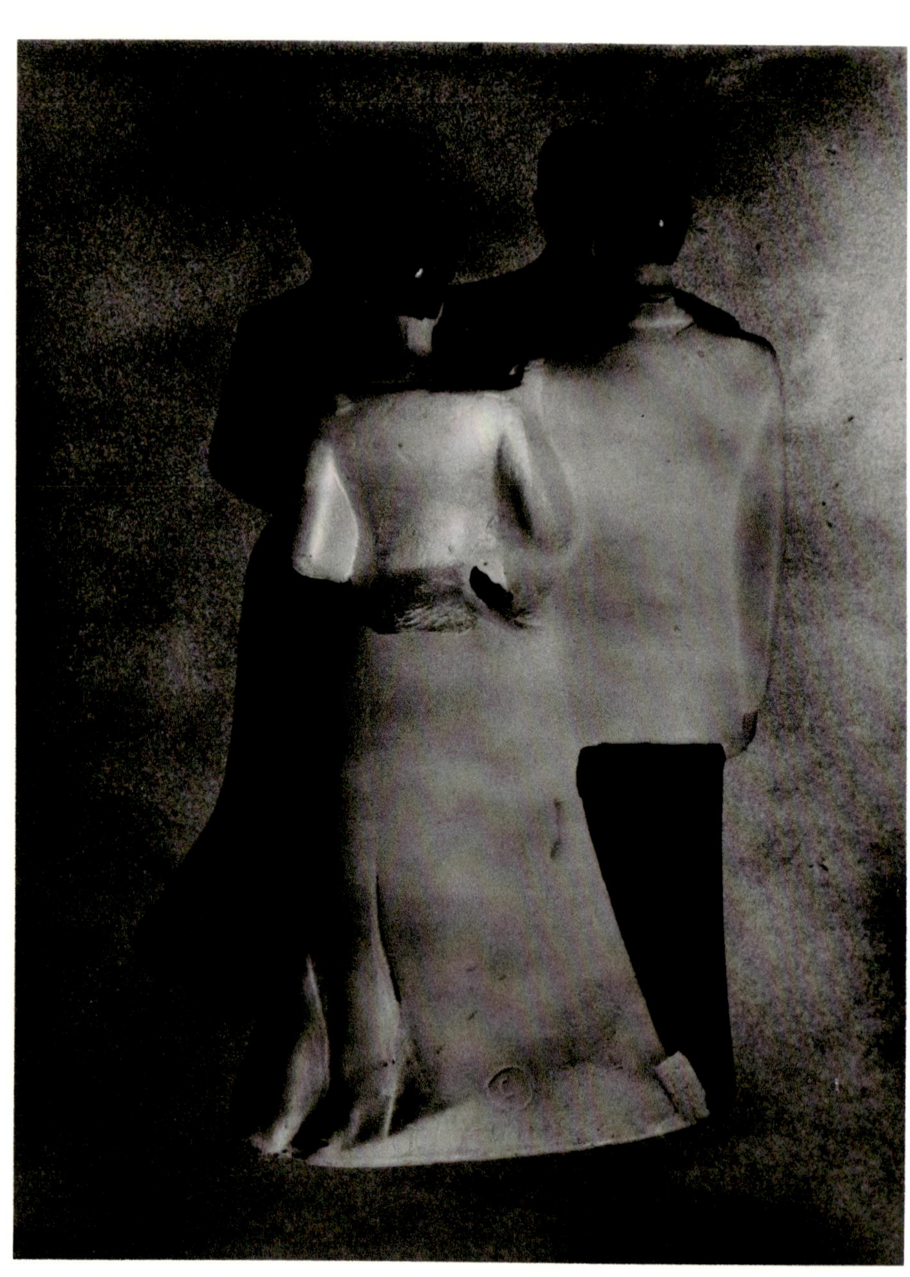

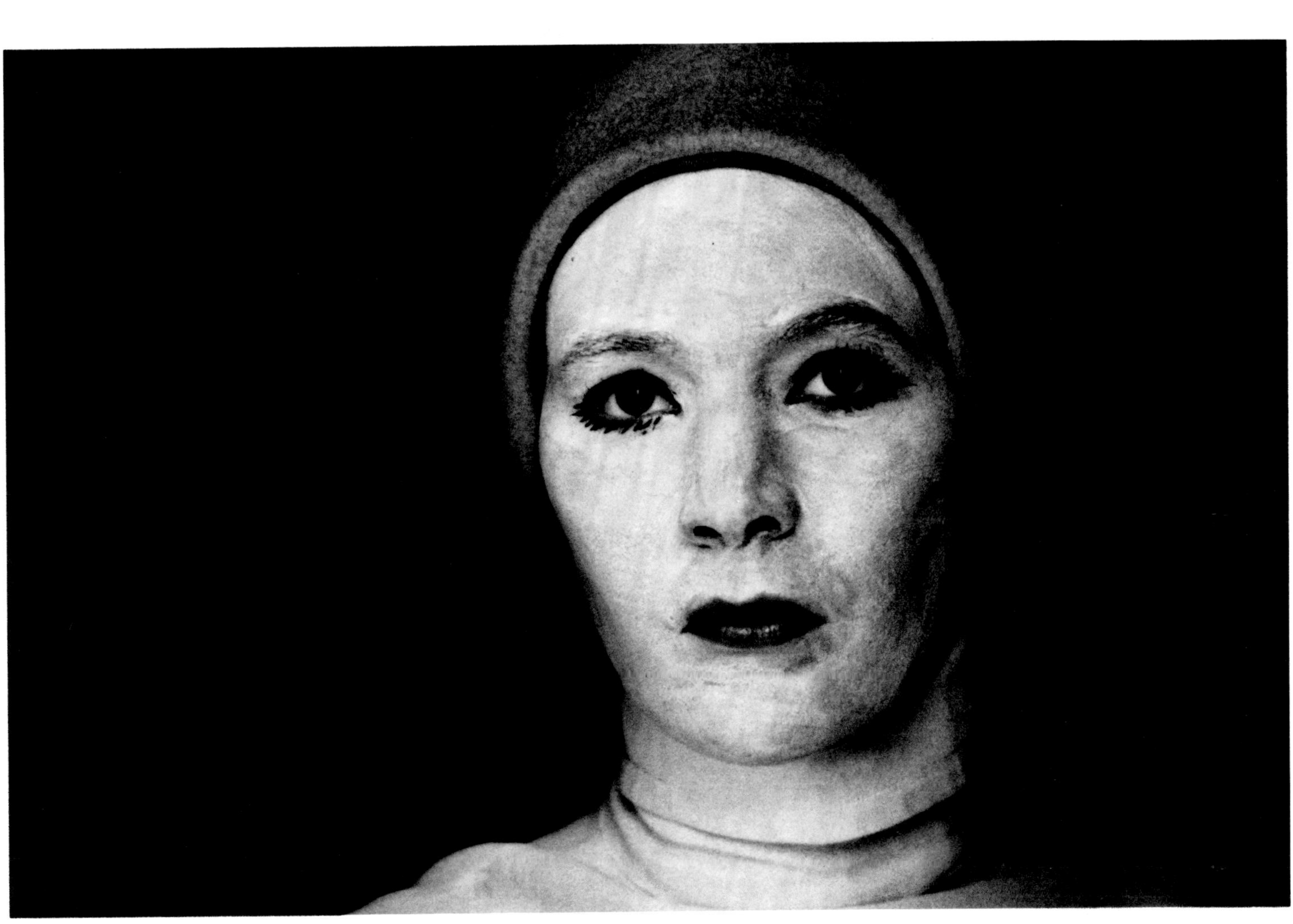

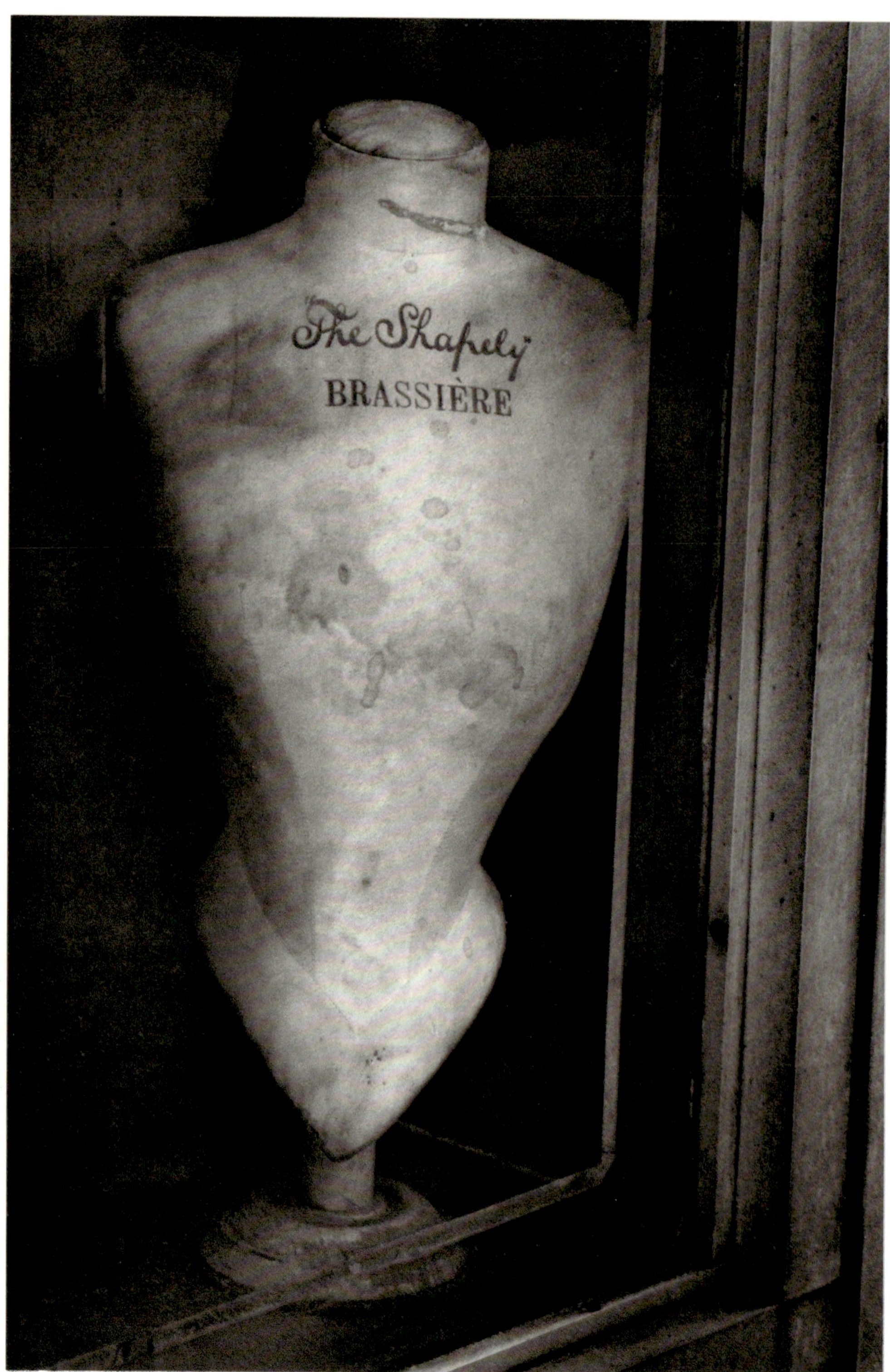
The Shapely
BRASSIÈRE

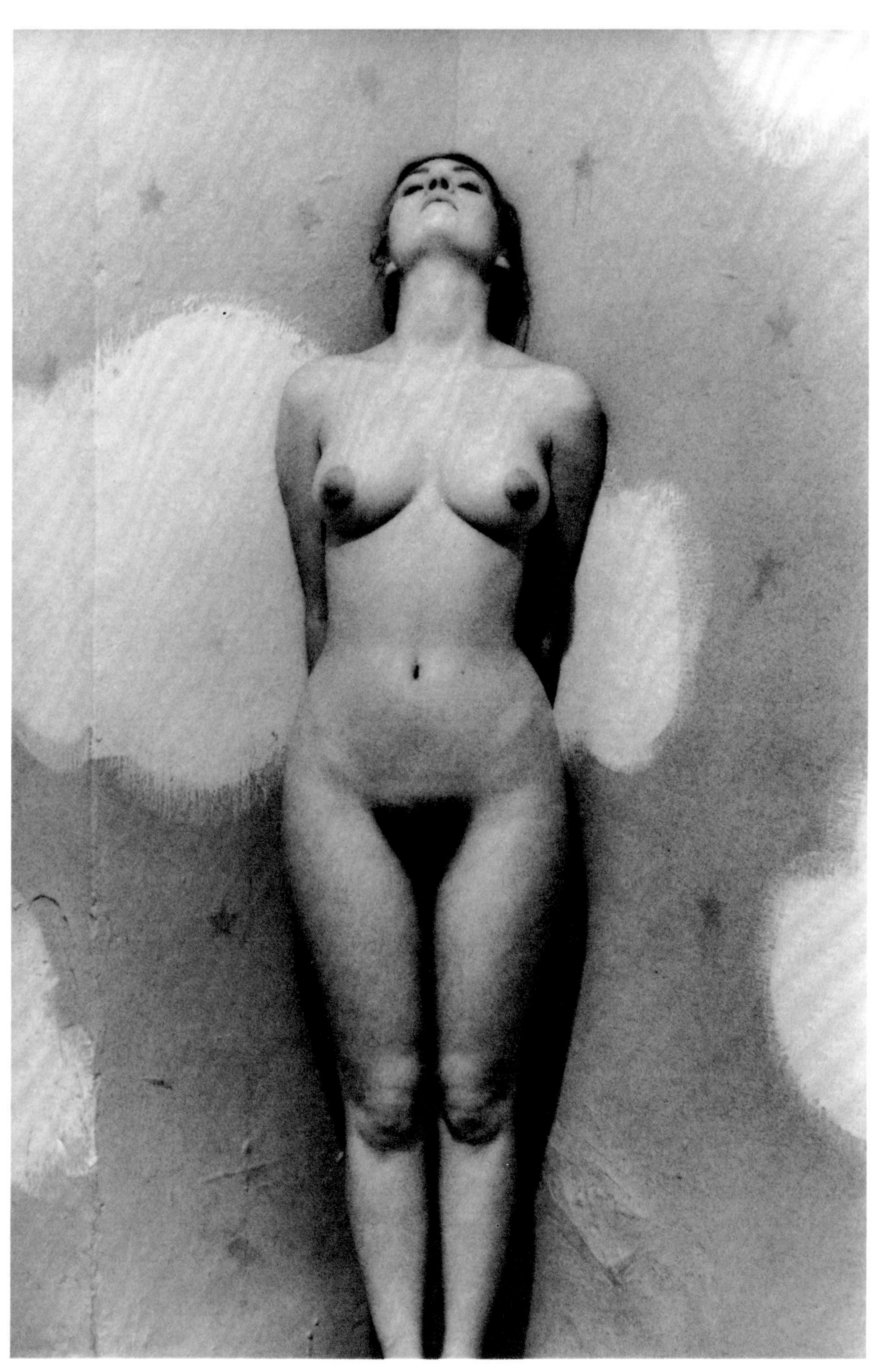

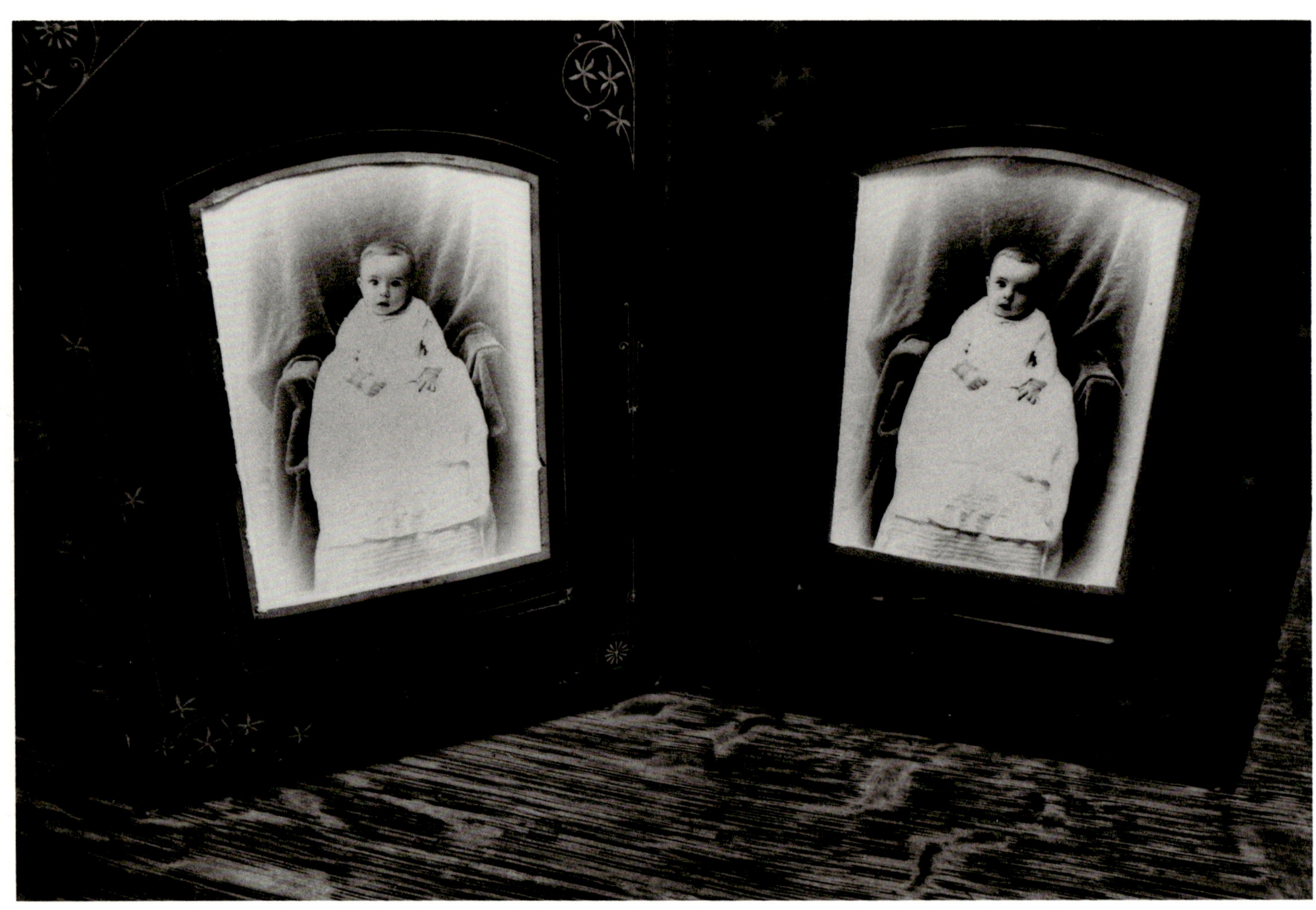

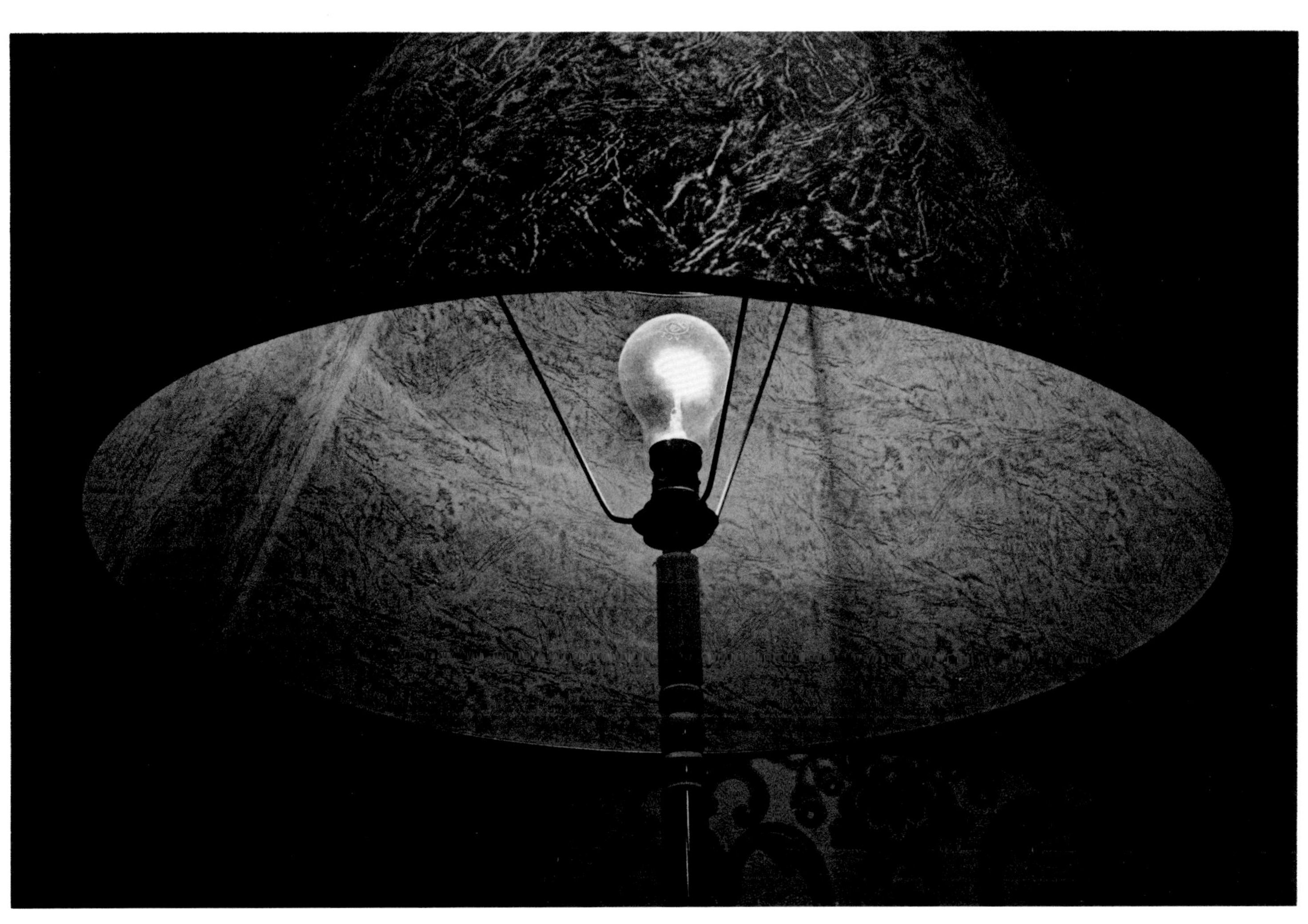

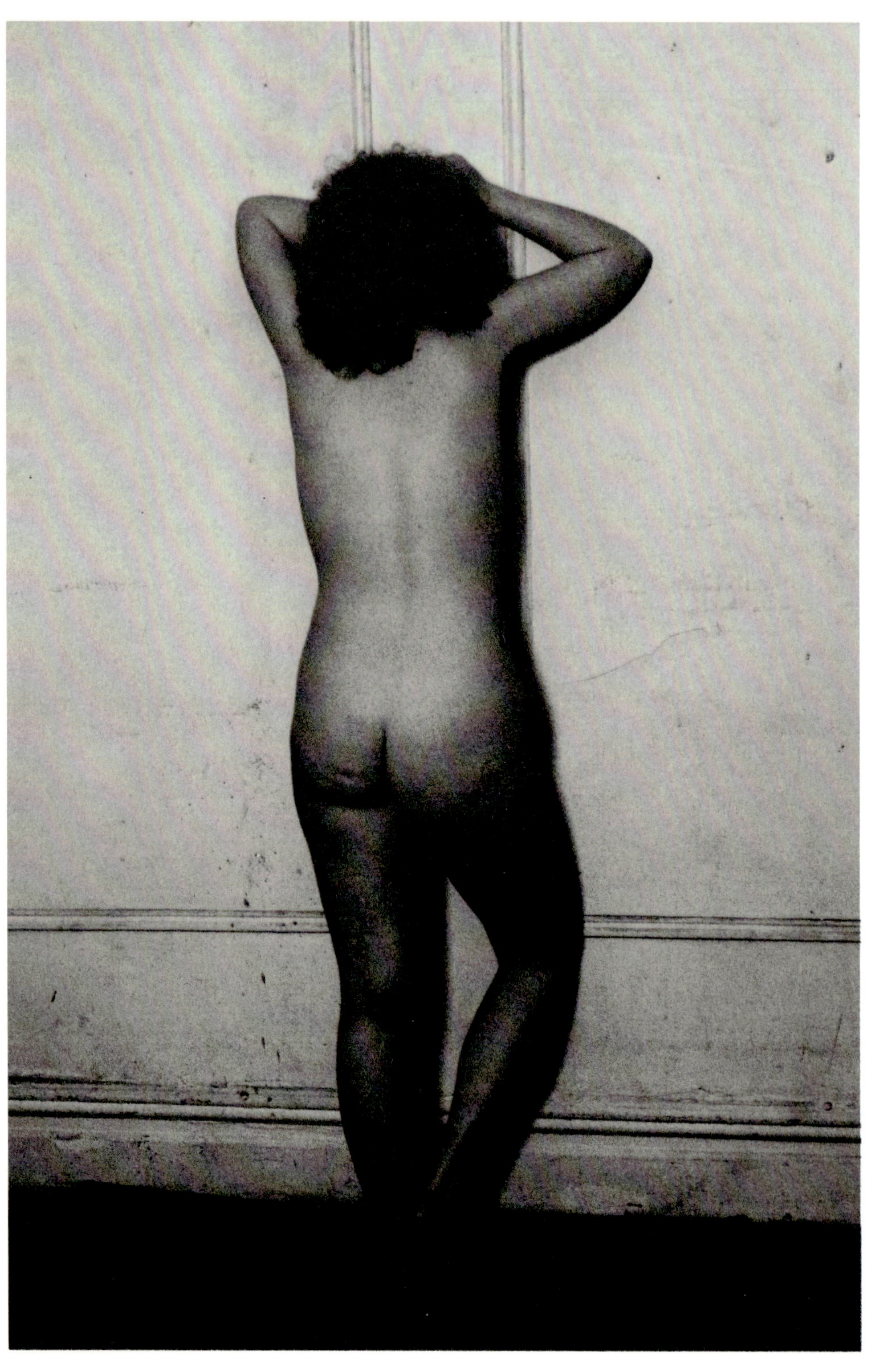

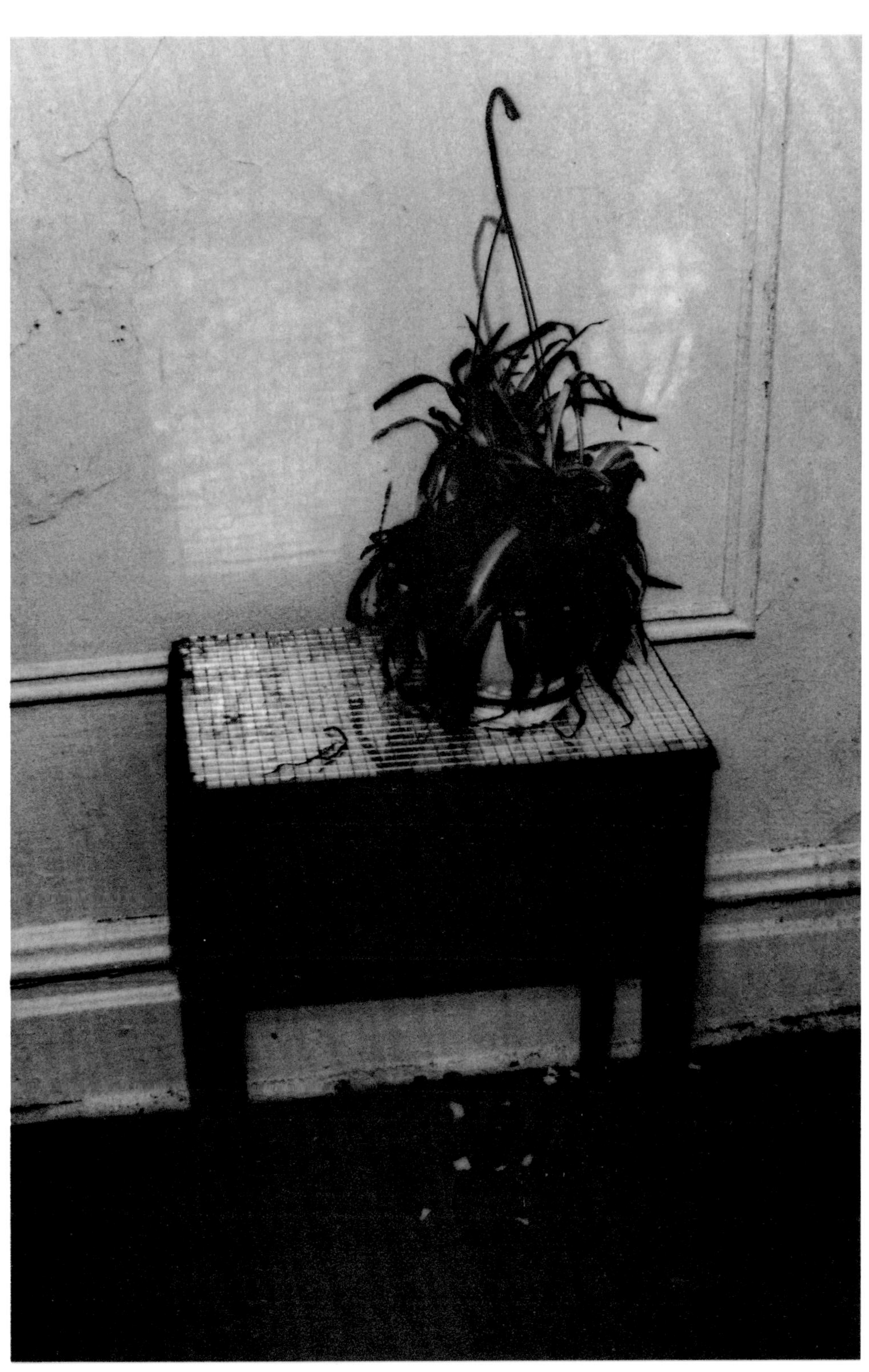

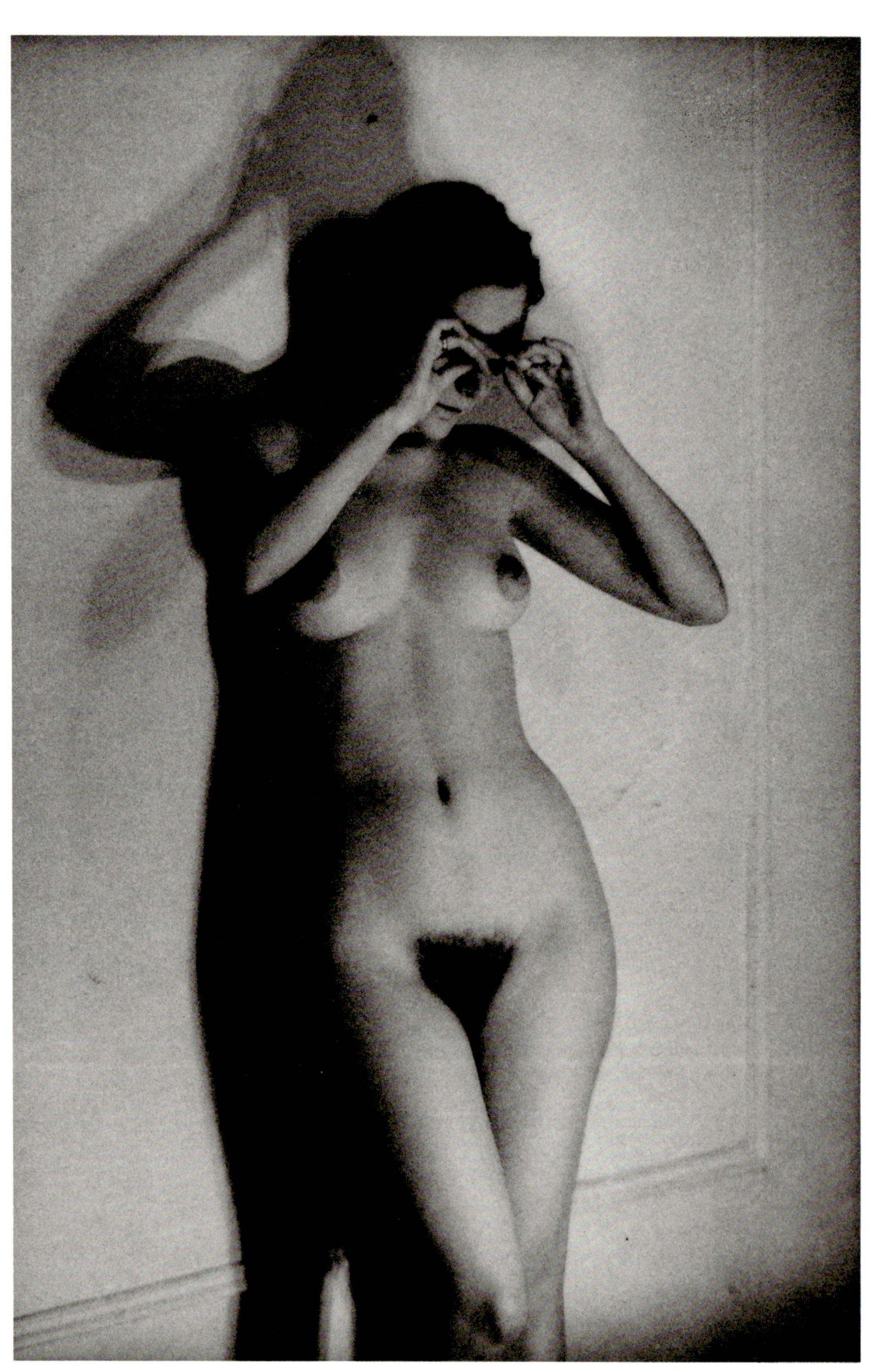

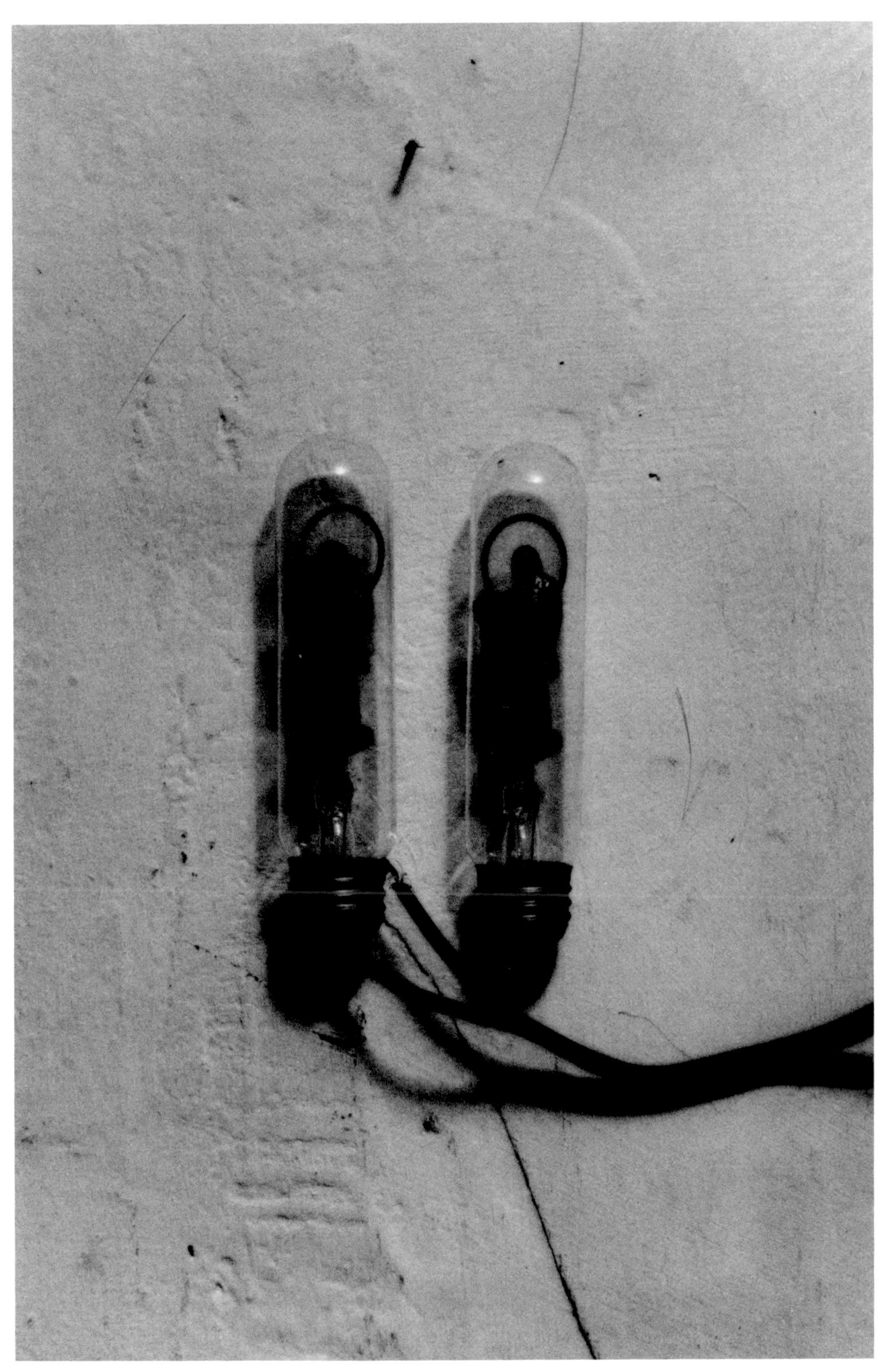

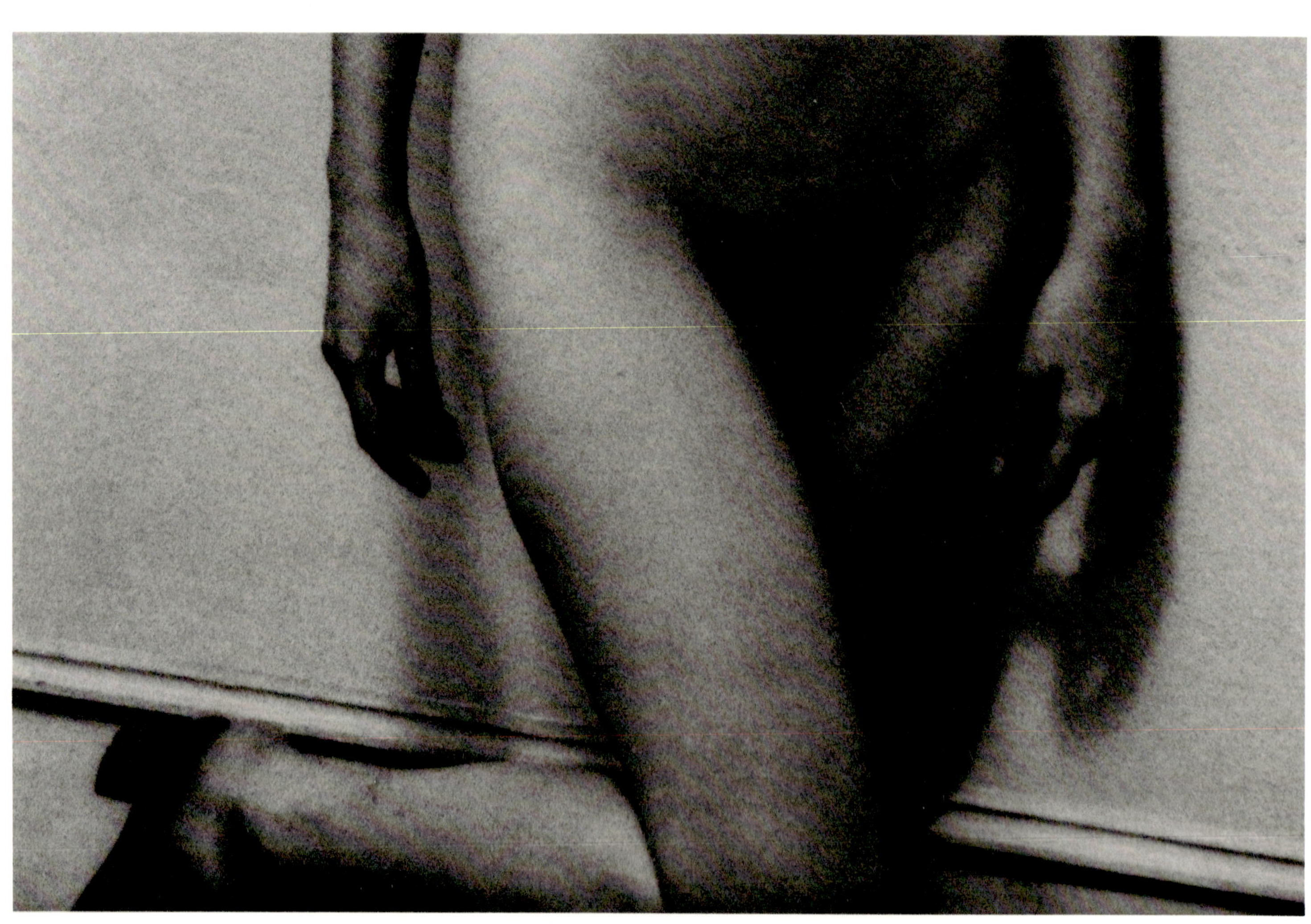

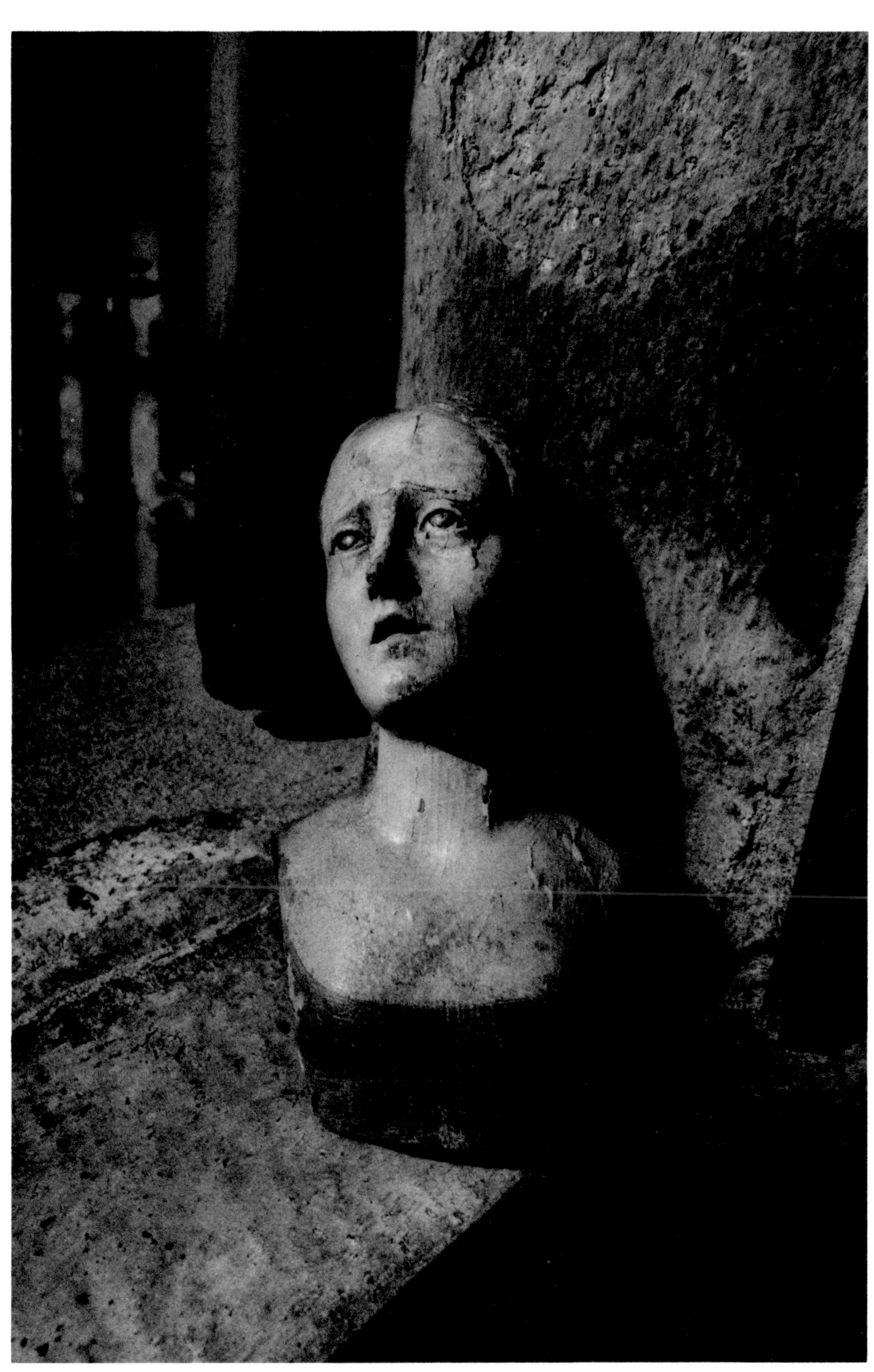

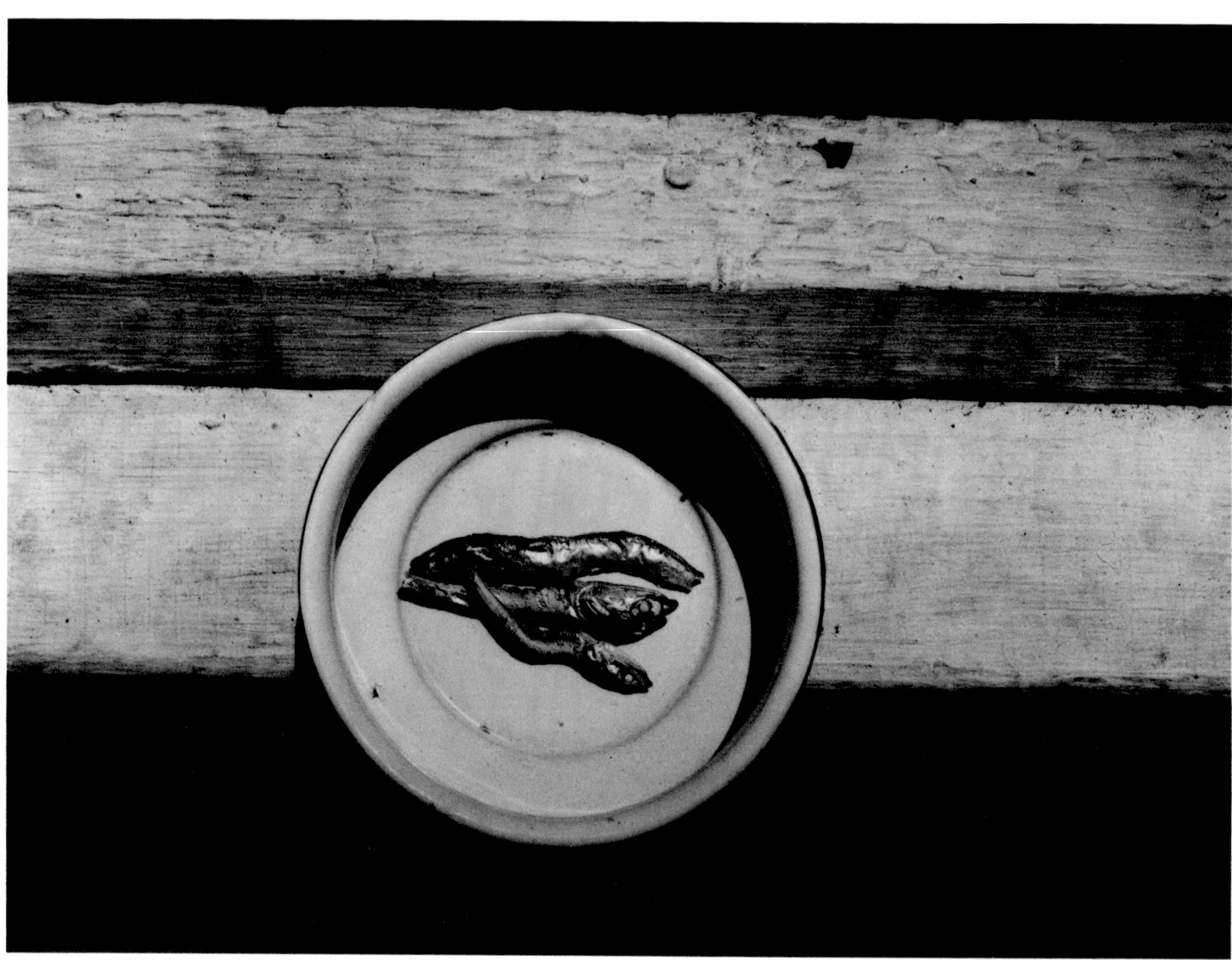

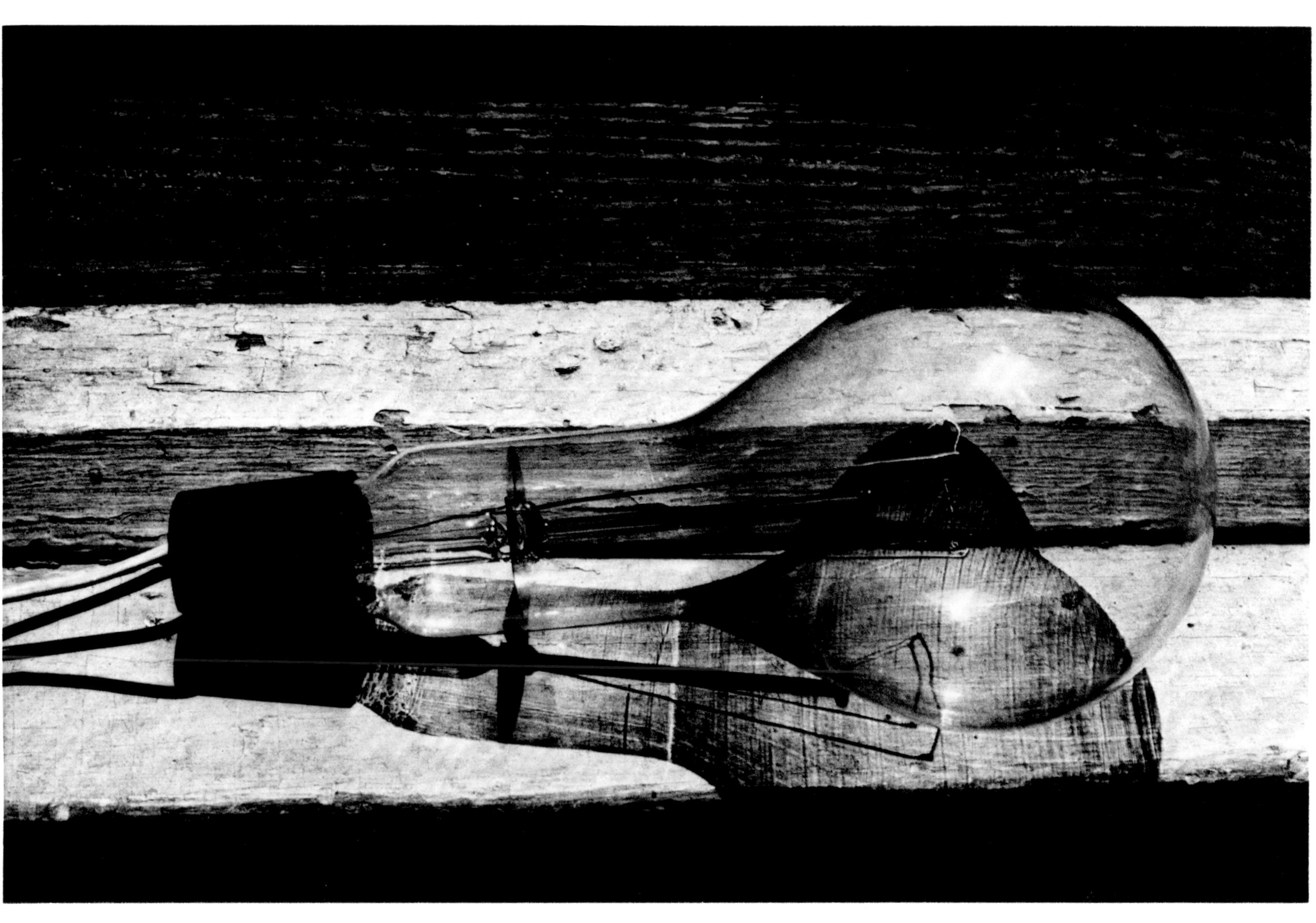

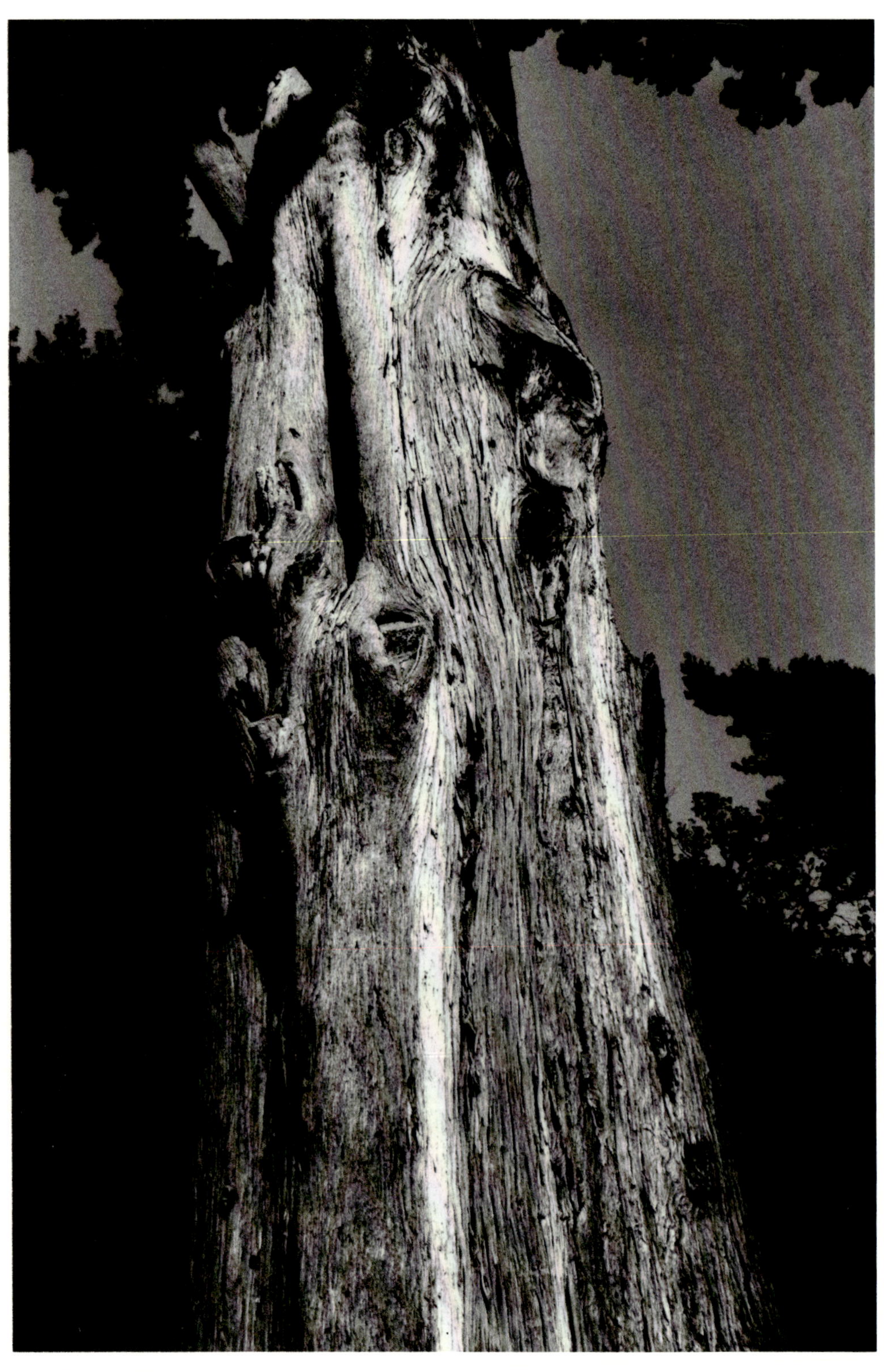

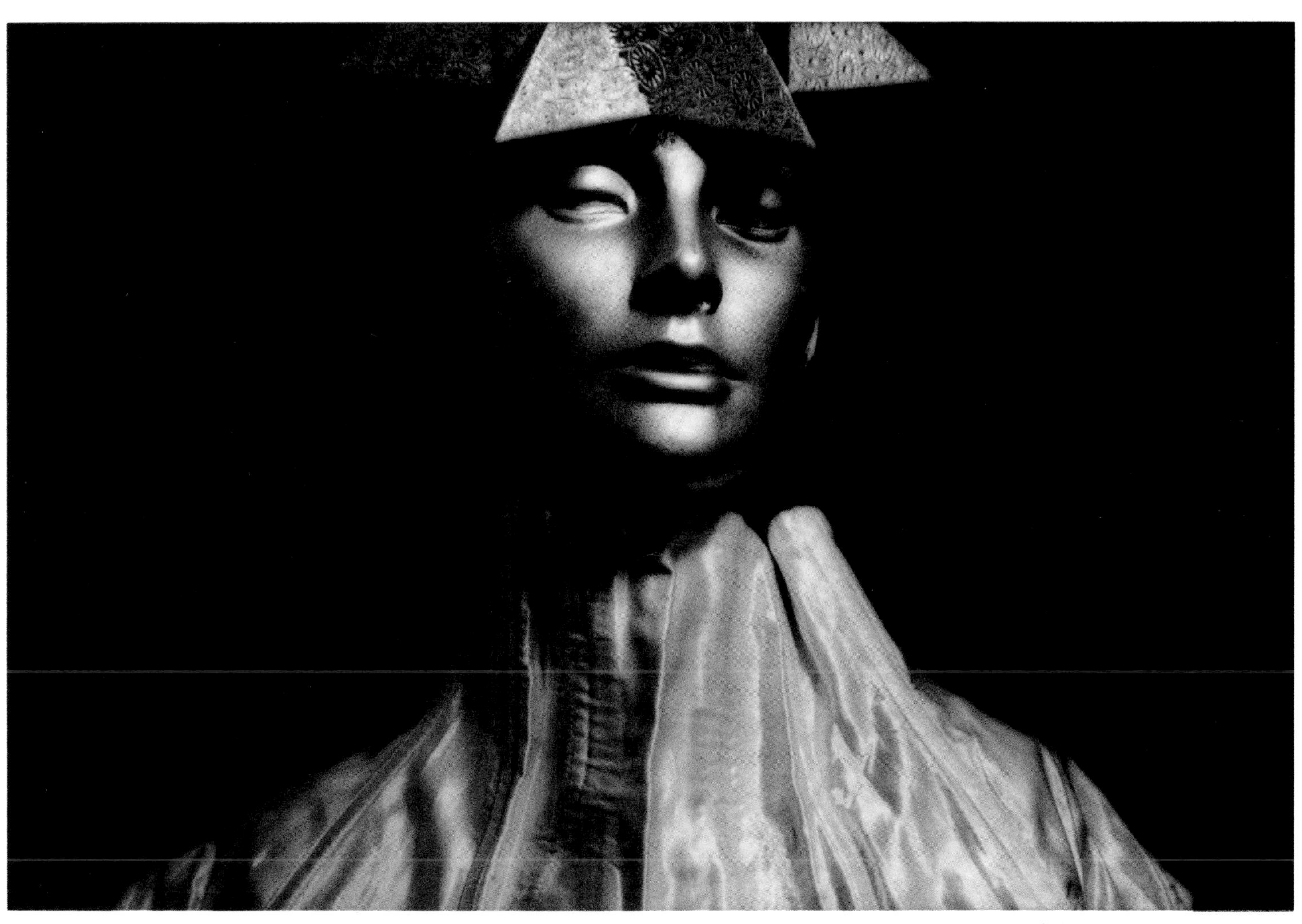

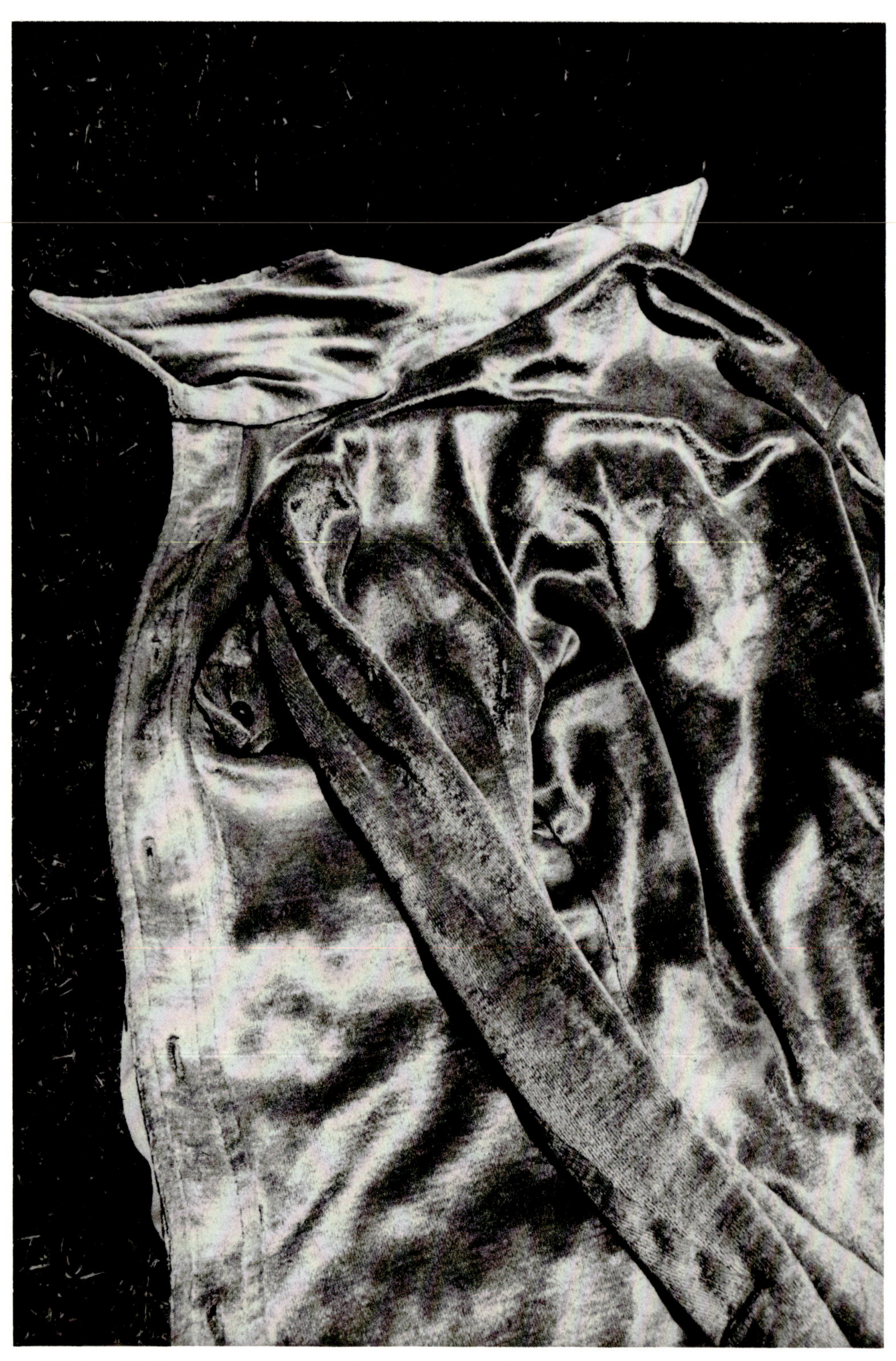

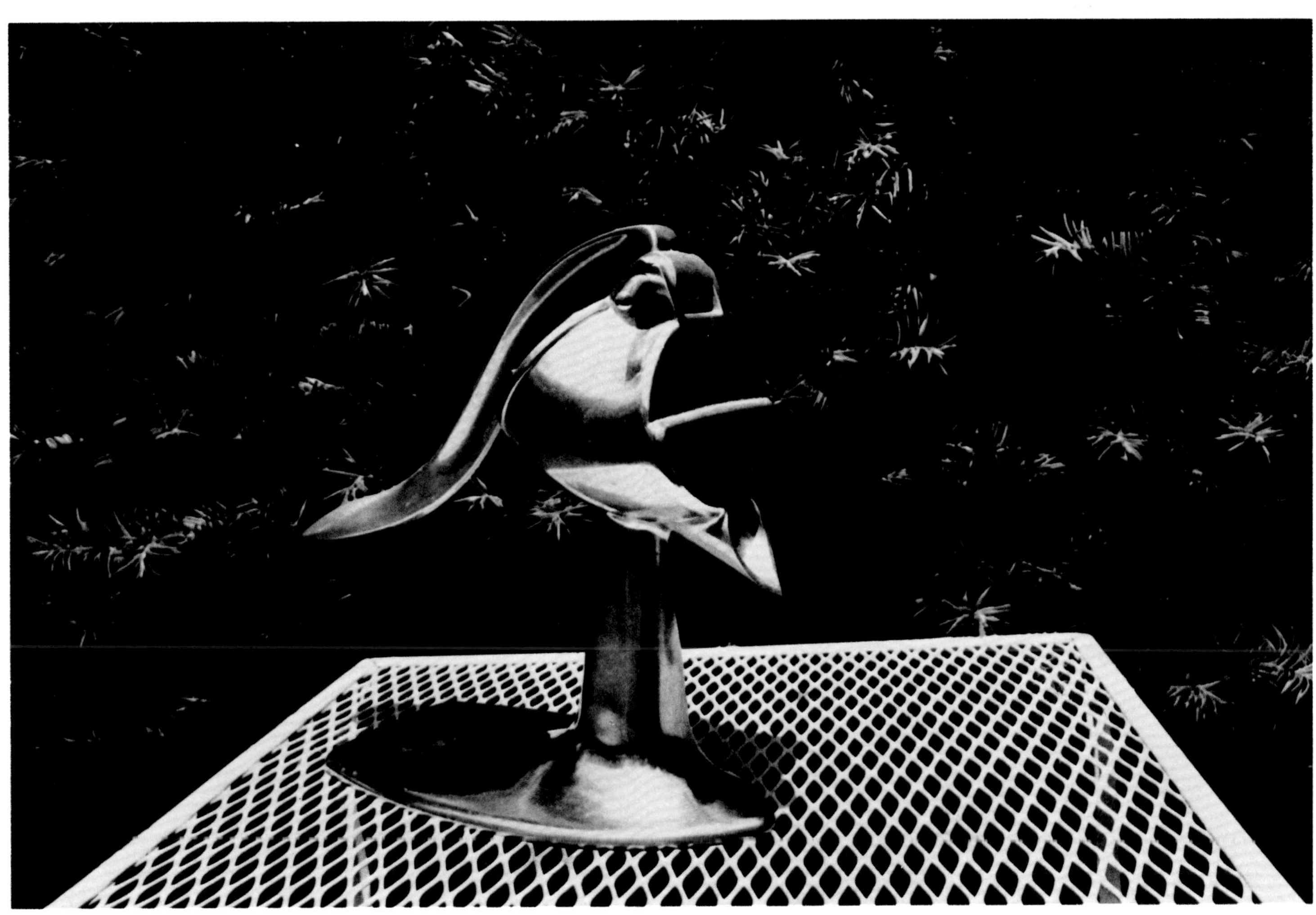

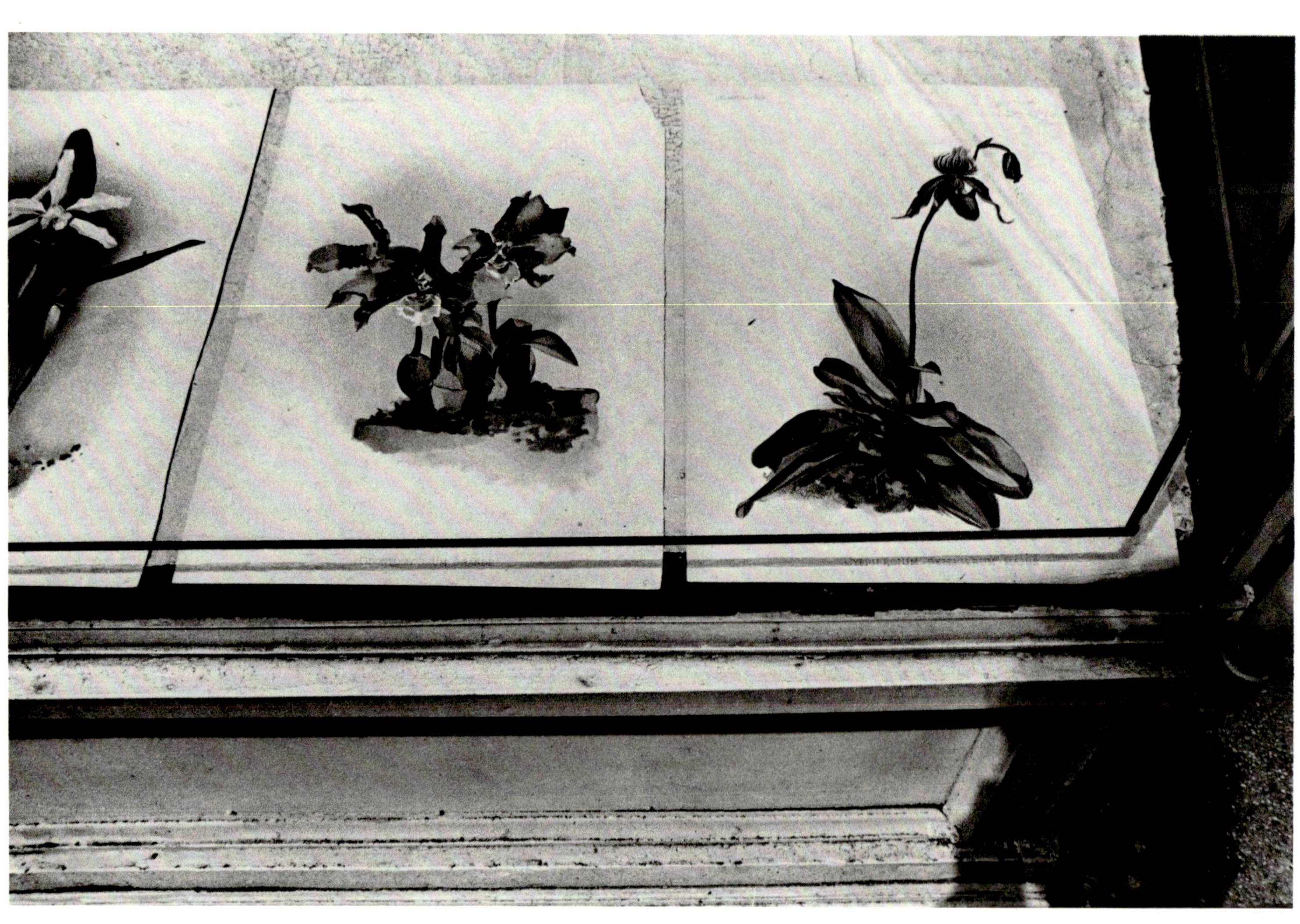

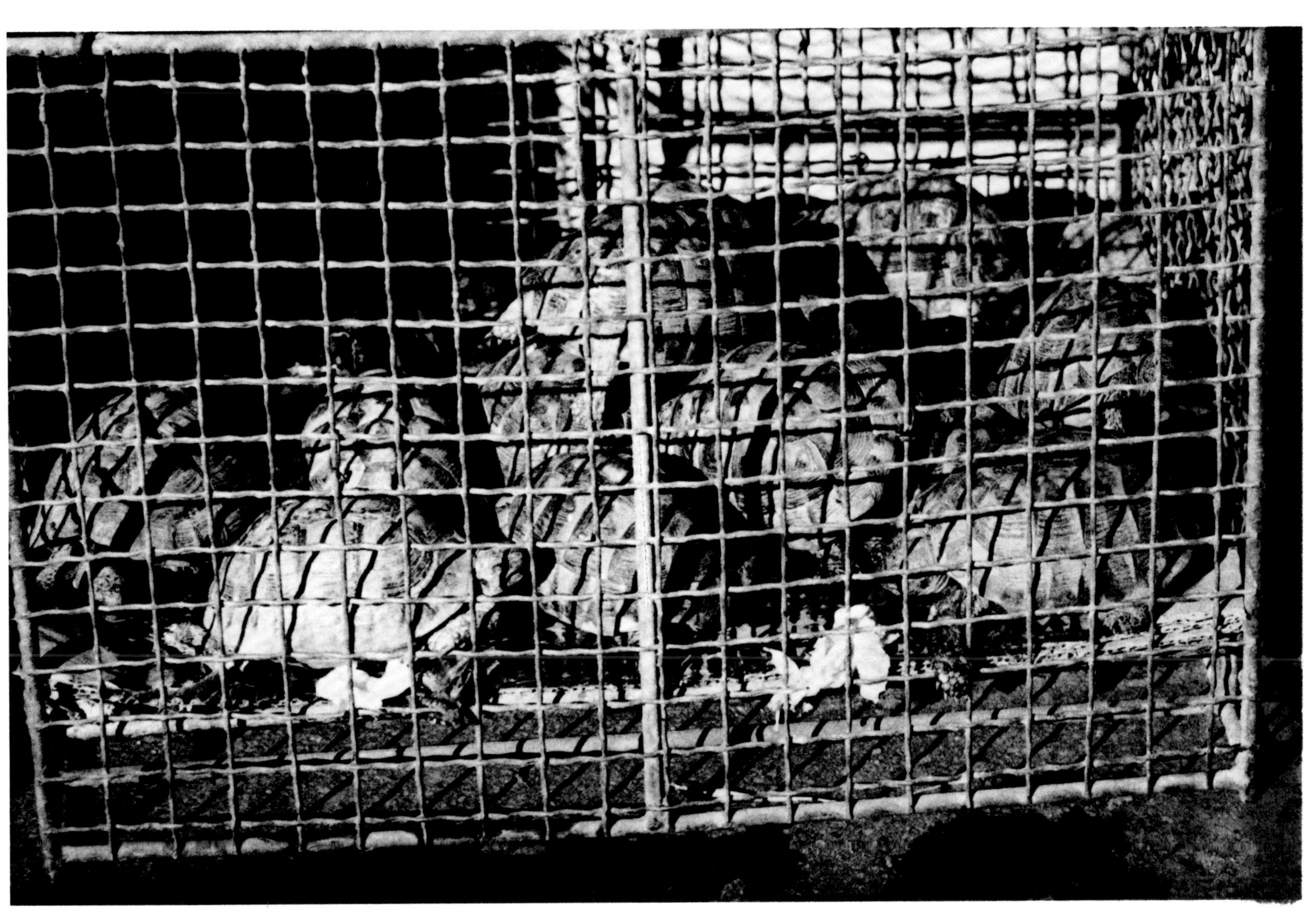

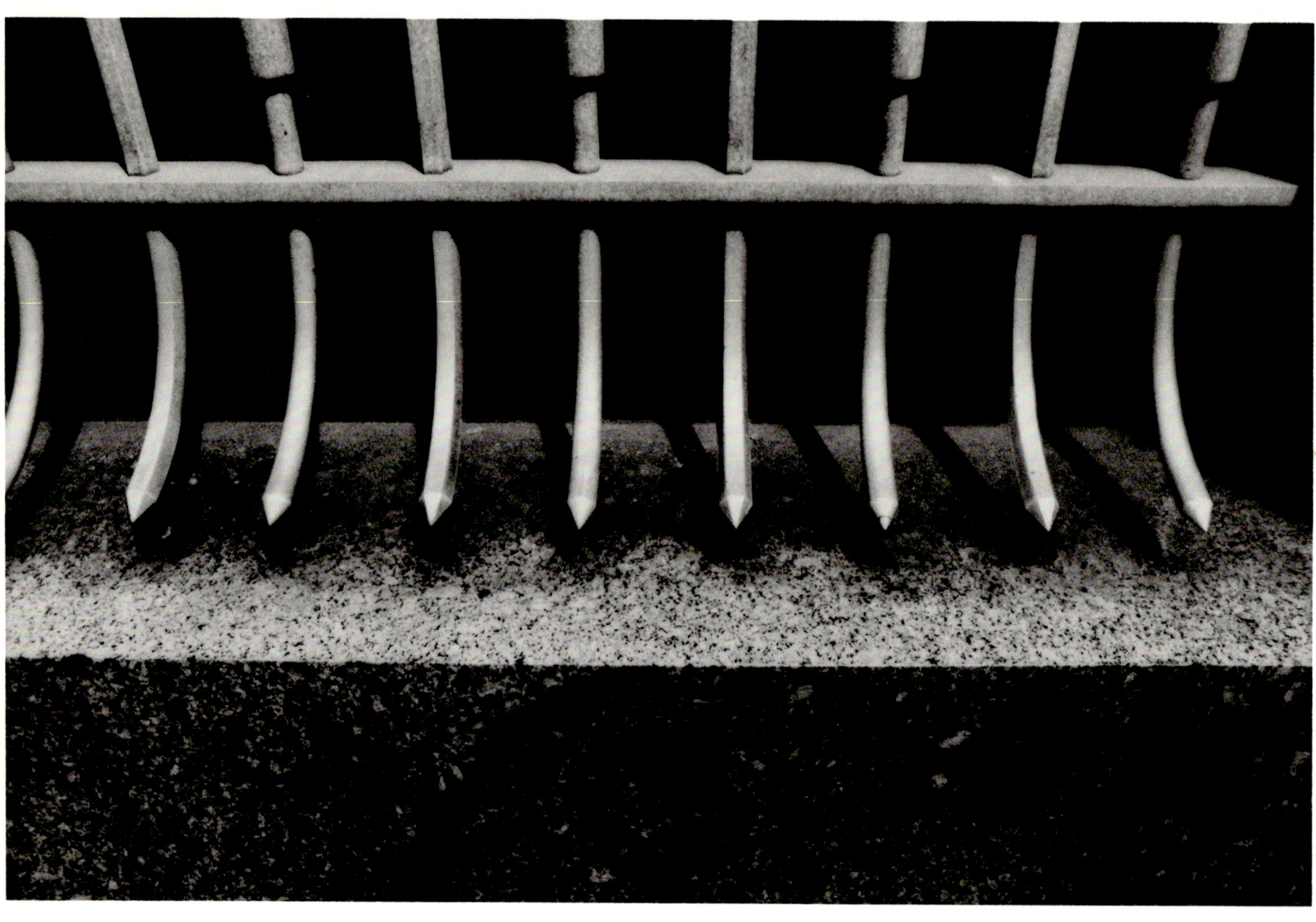

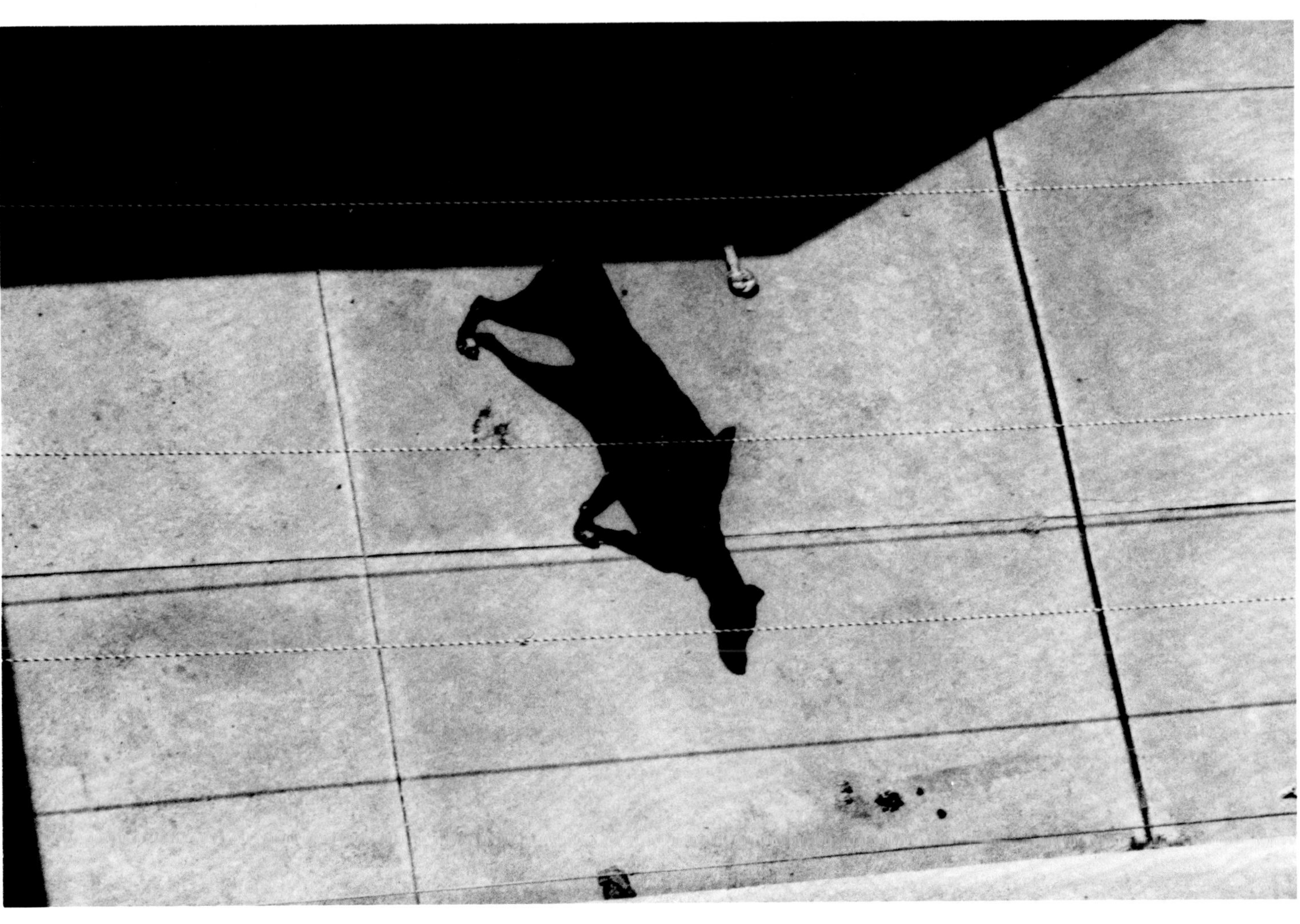

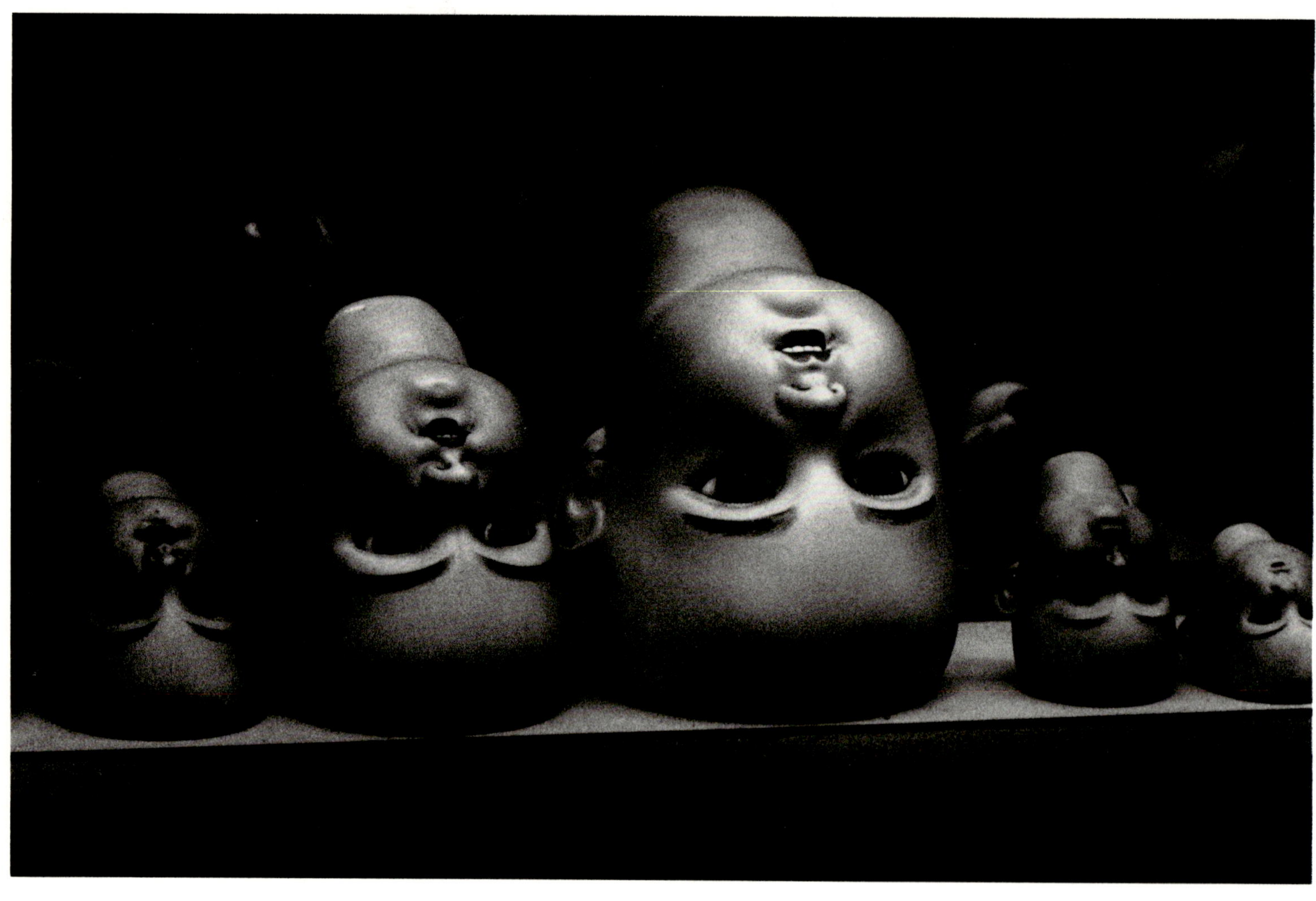

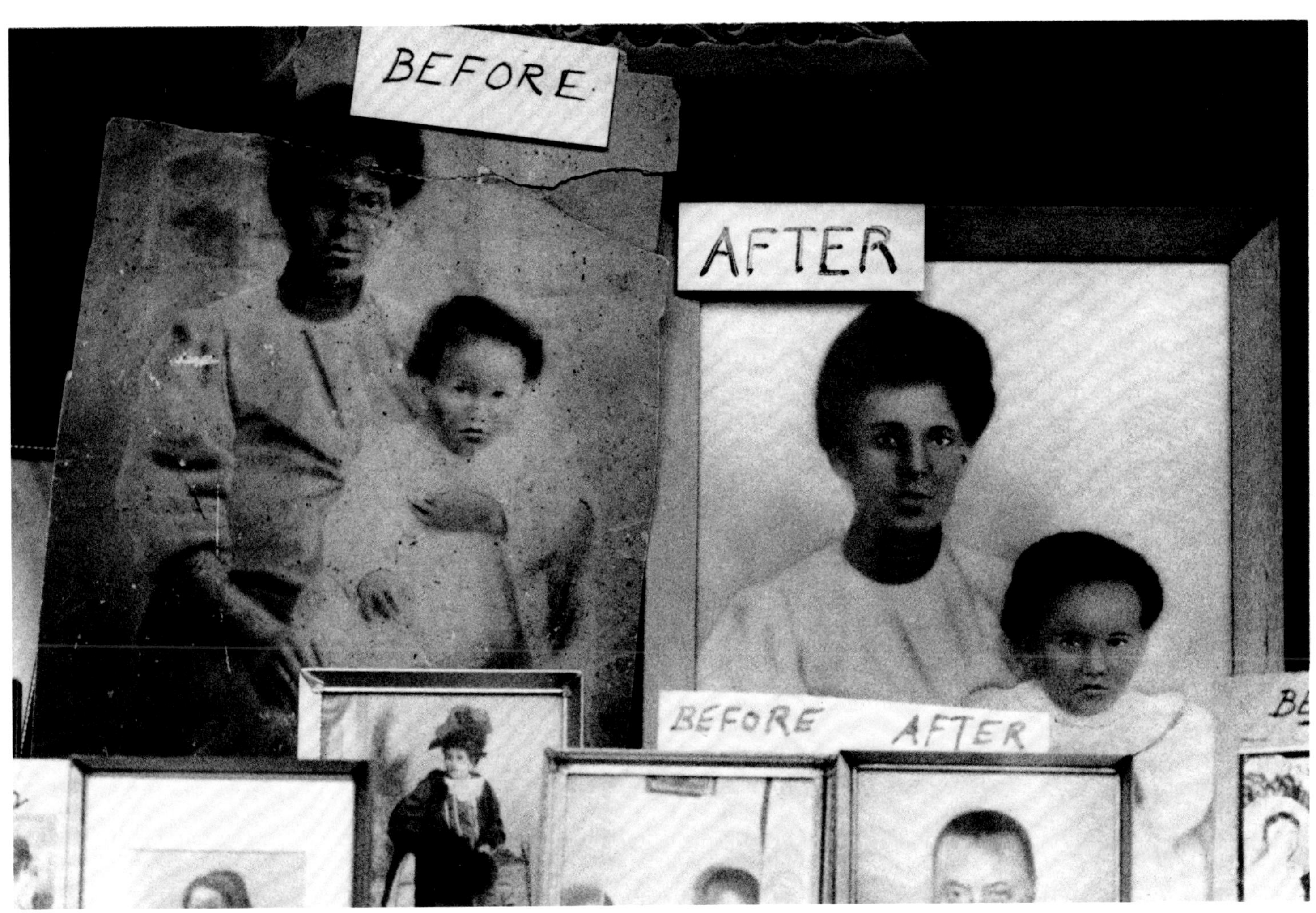
BEFORE
AFTER
BEFORE
AFTER

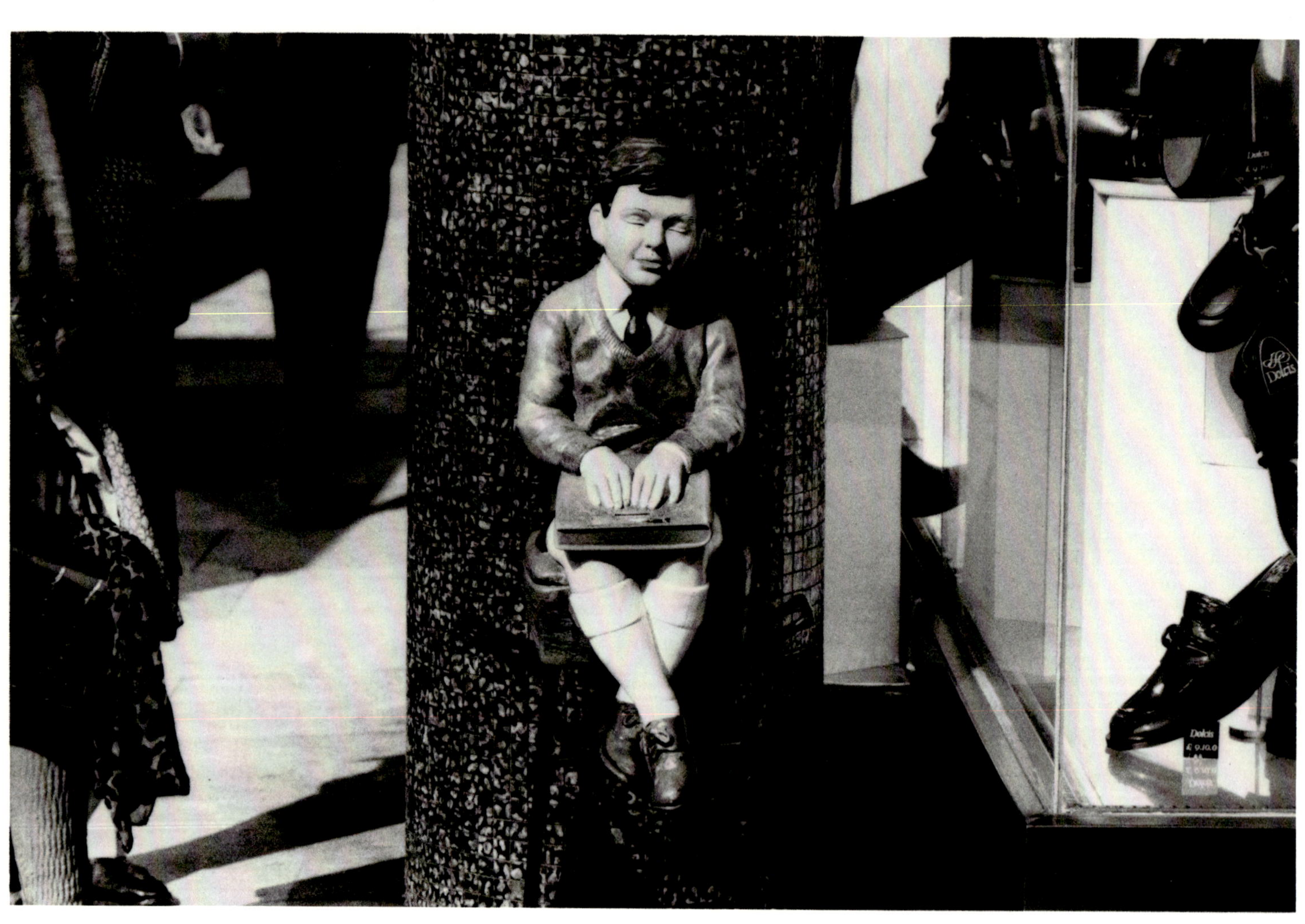
Dolcis
Dolcis
Dolcis
£ 9.10.0

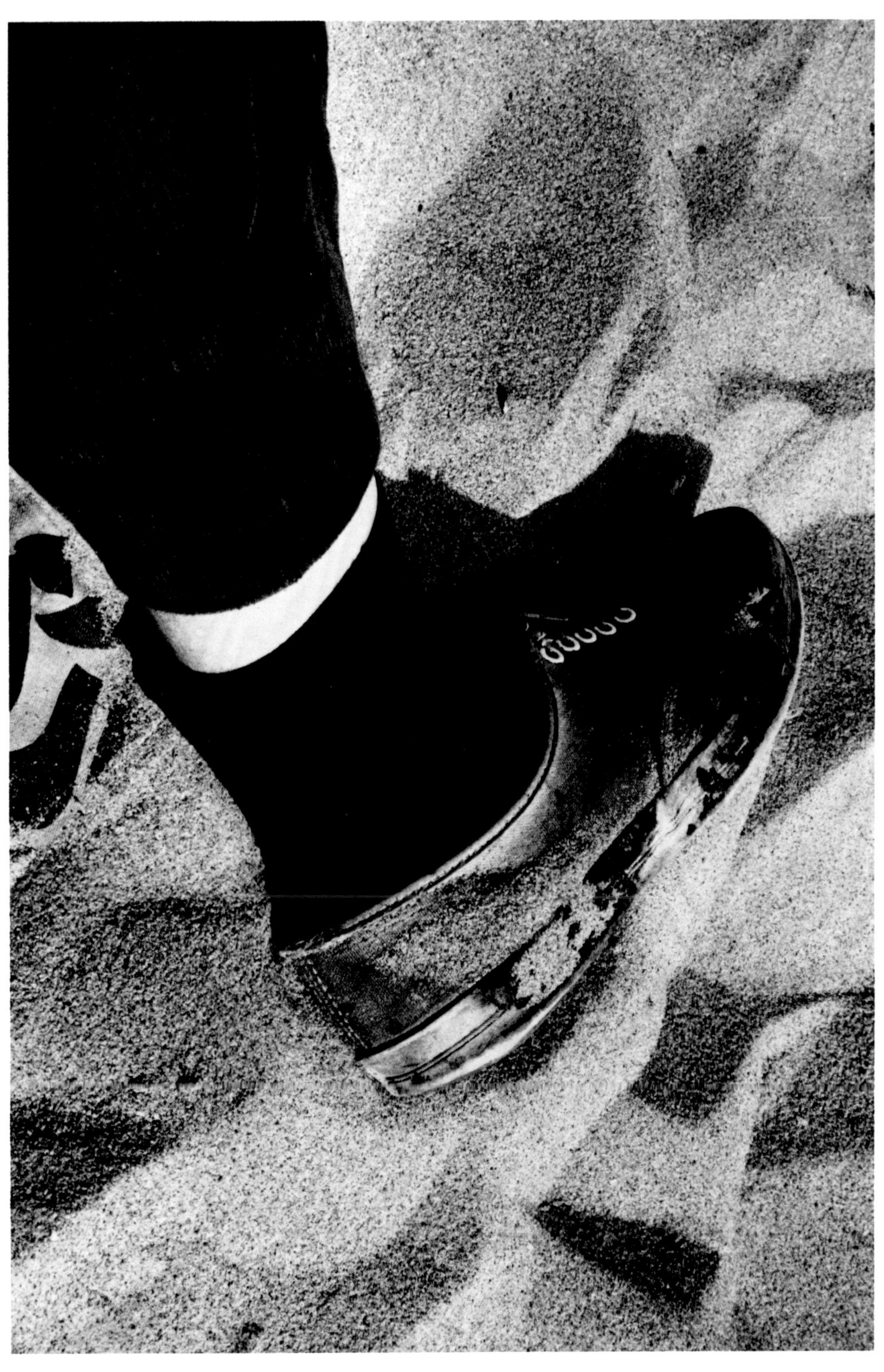

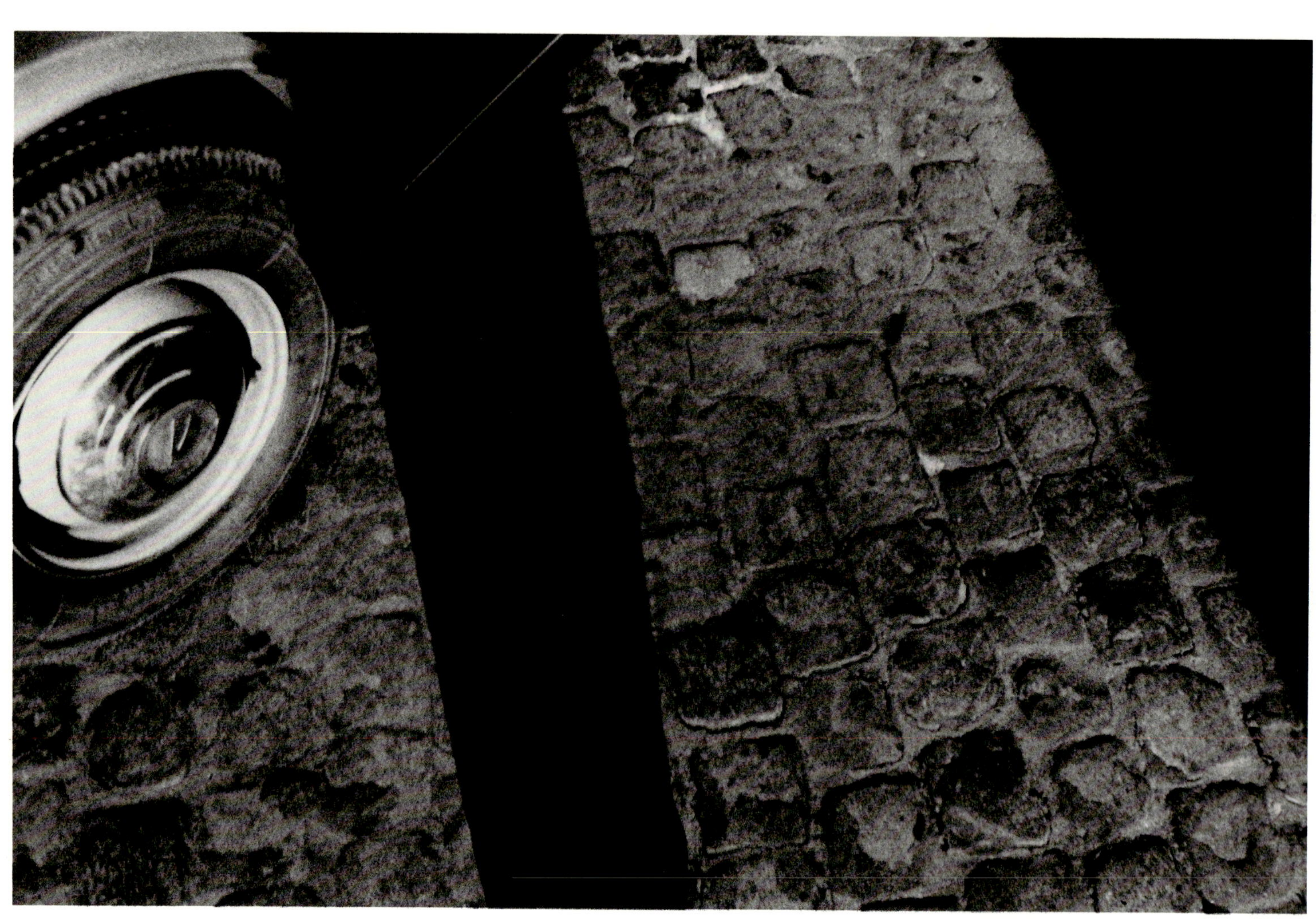

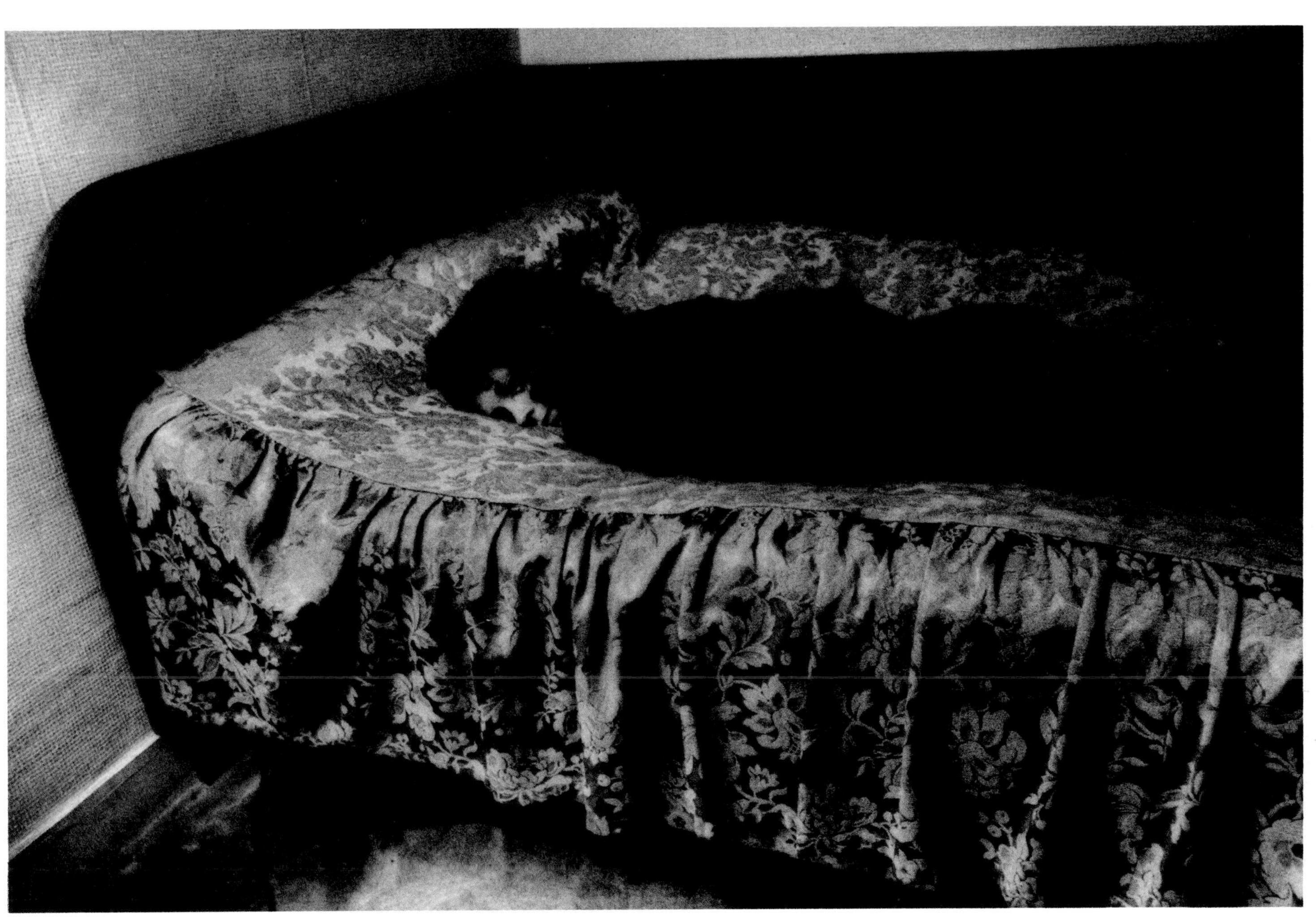

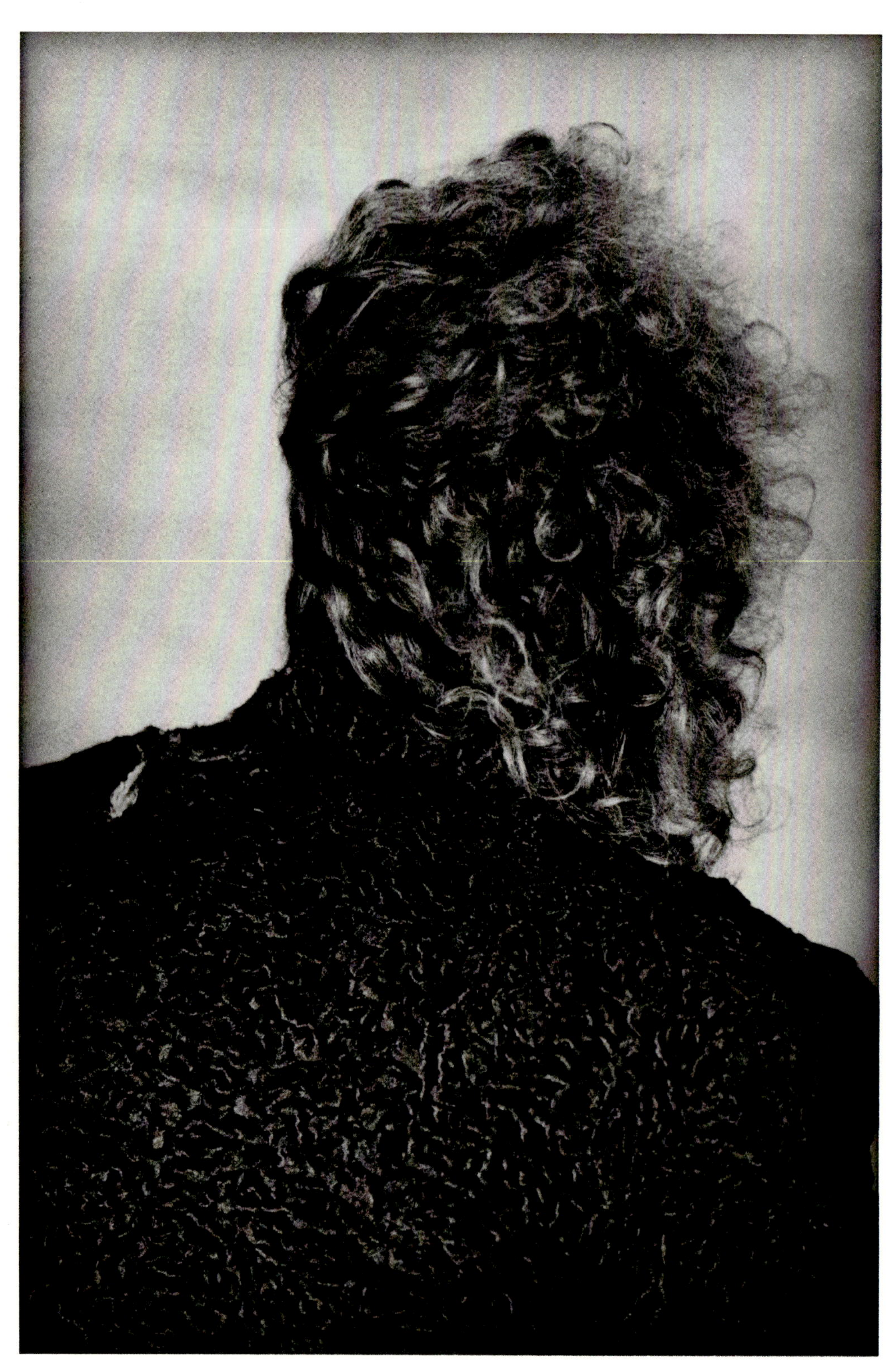

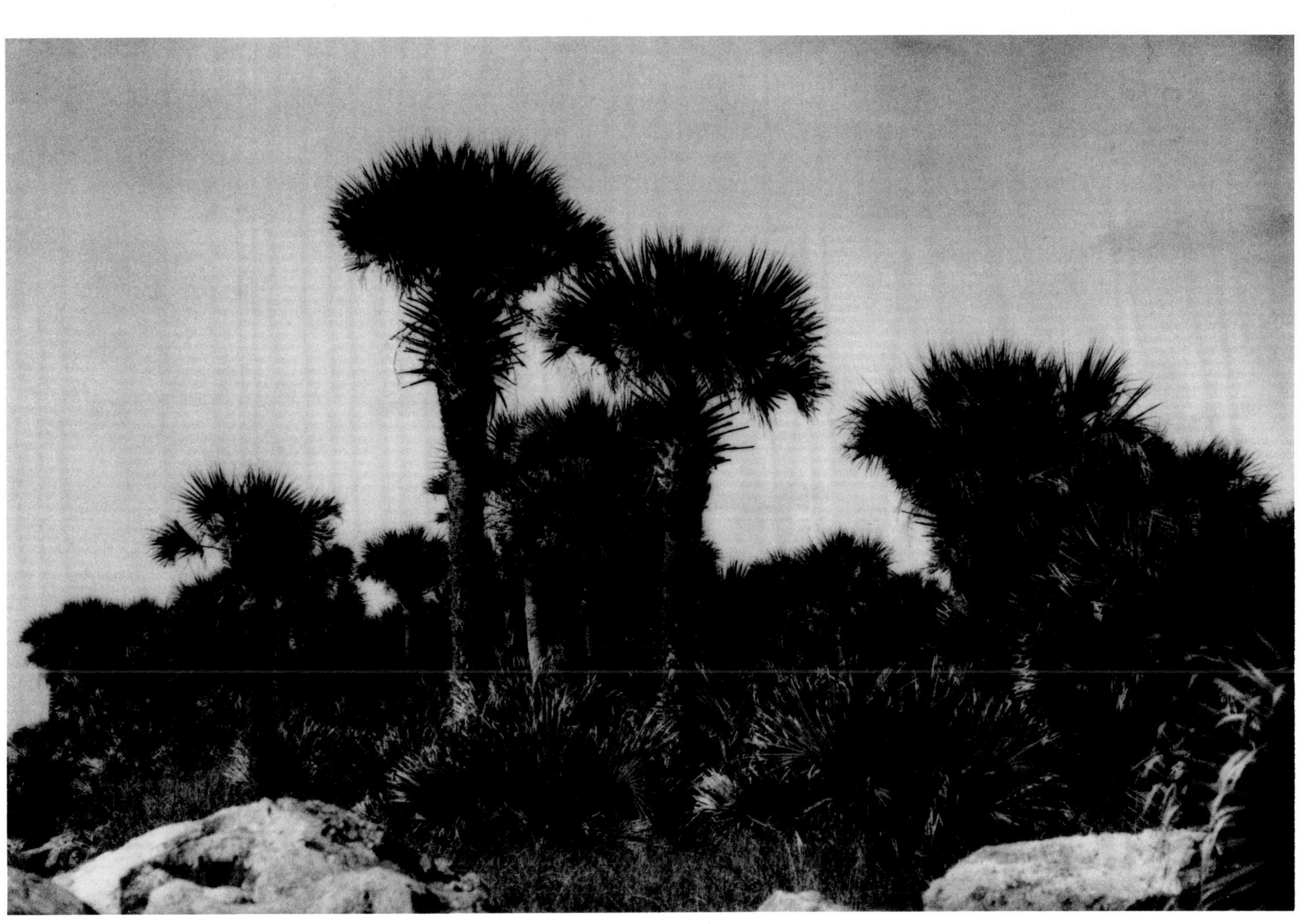

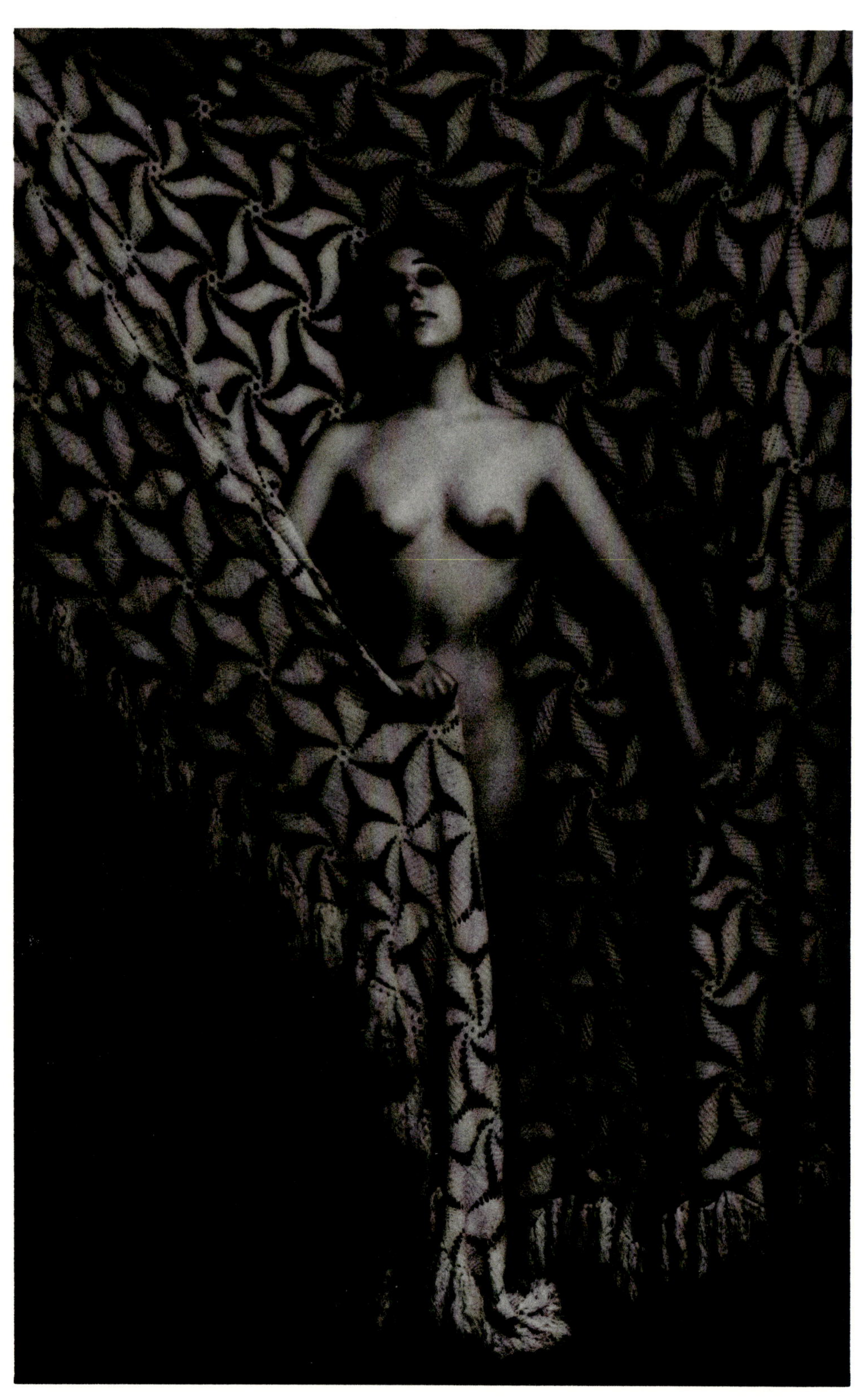

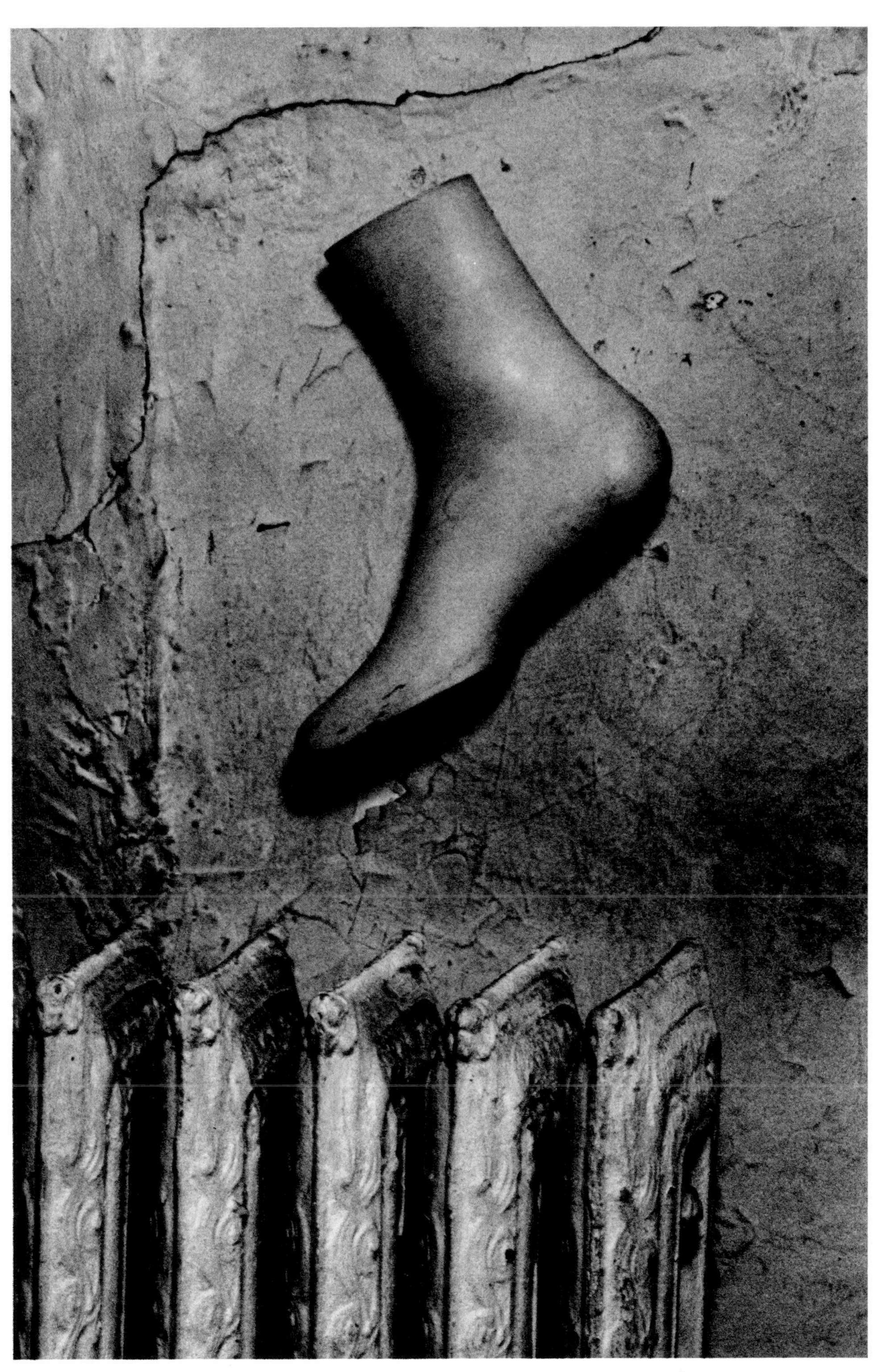

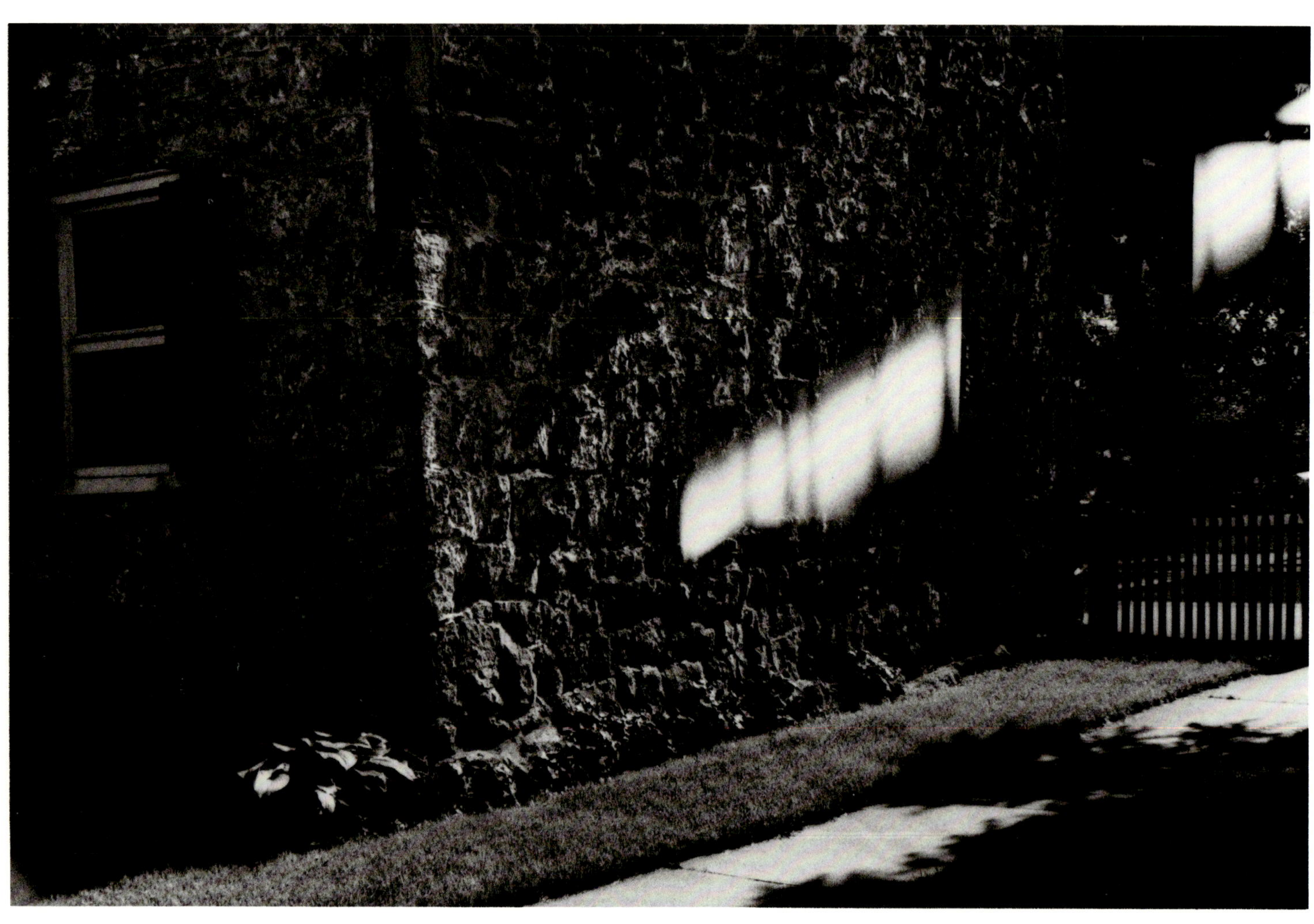

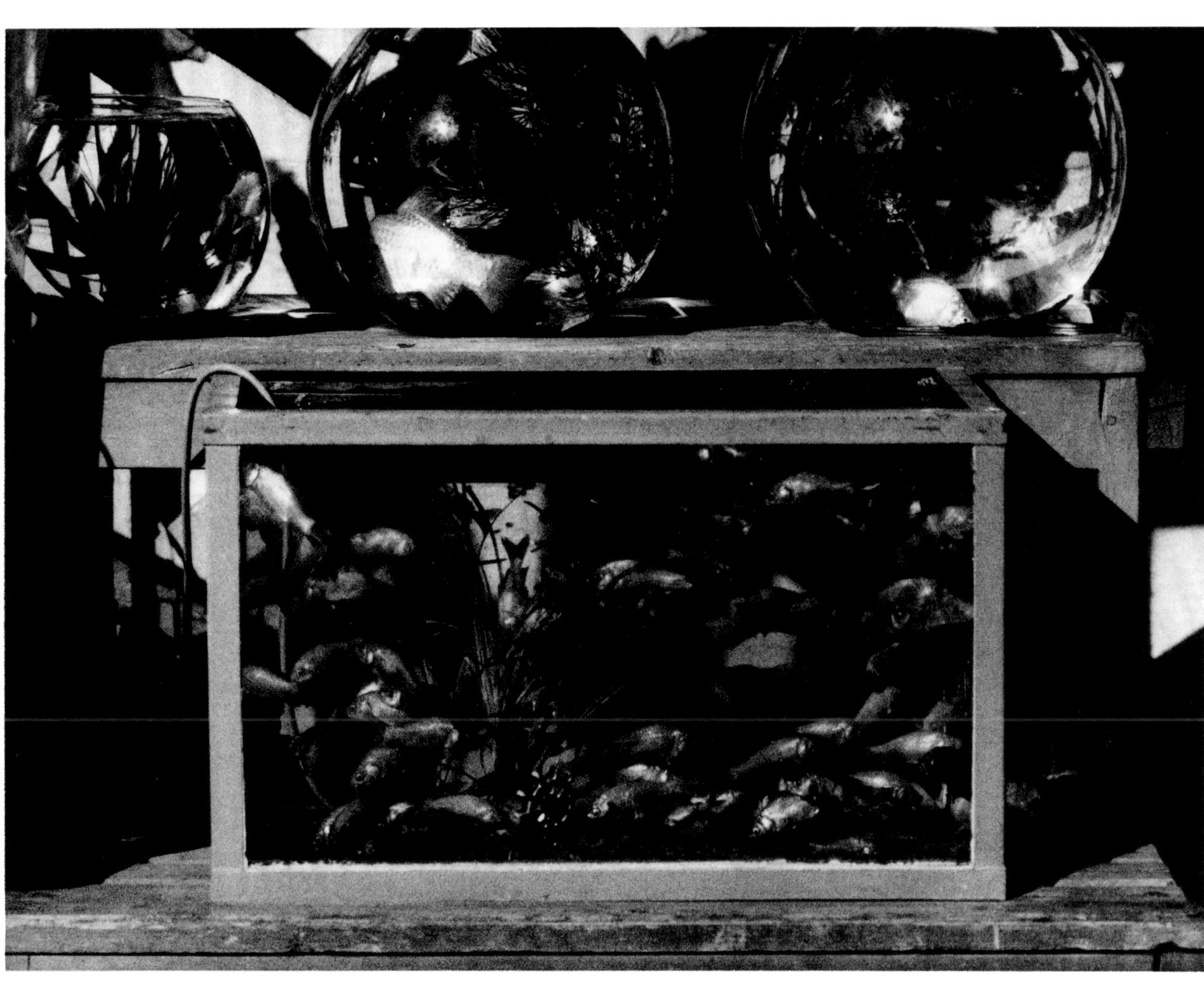

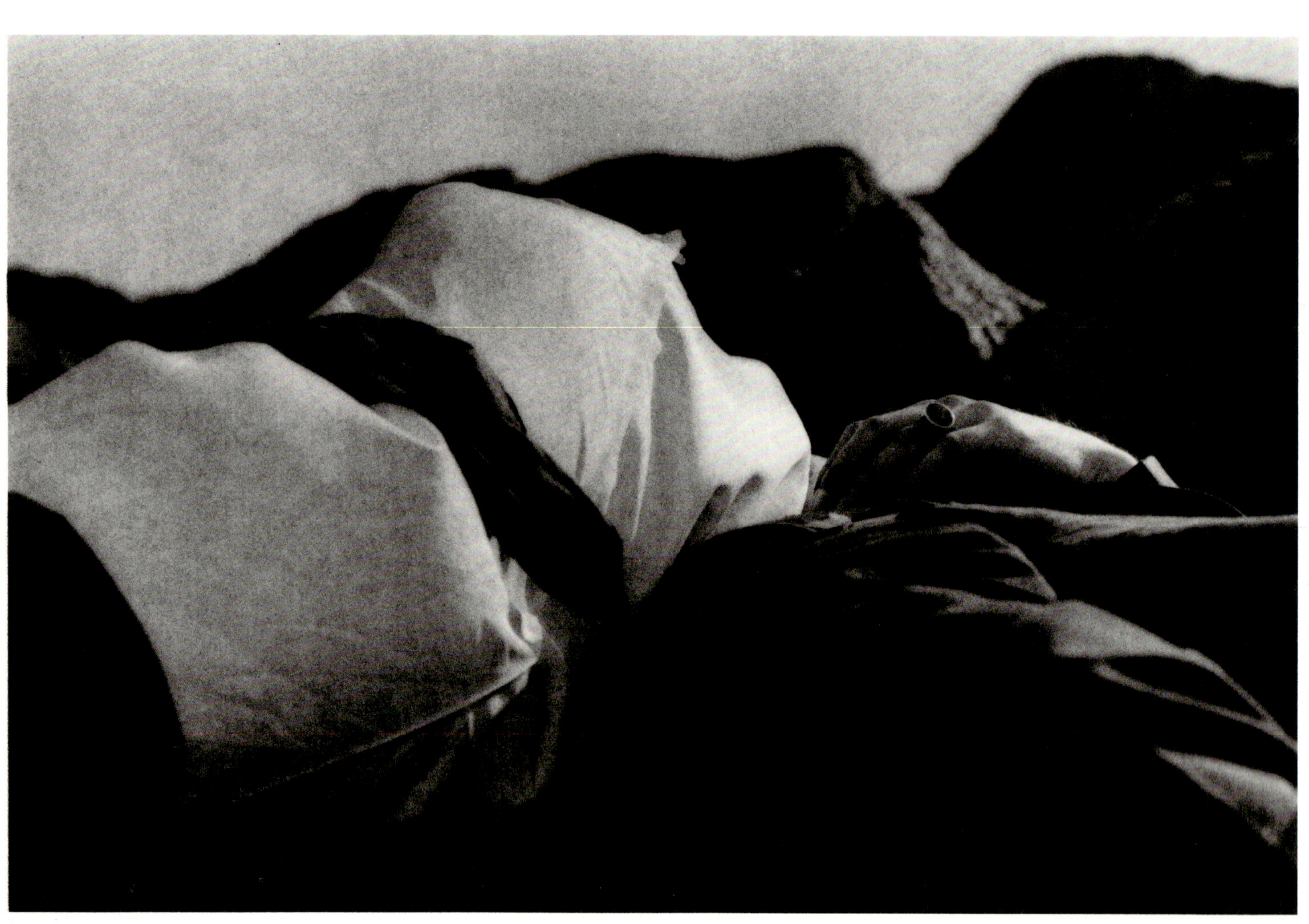

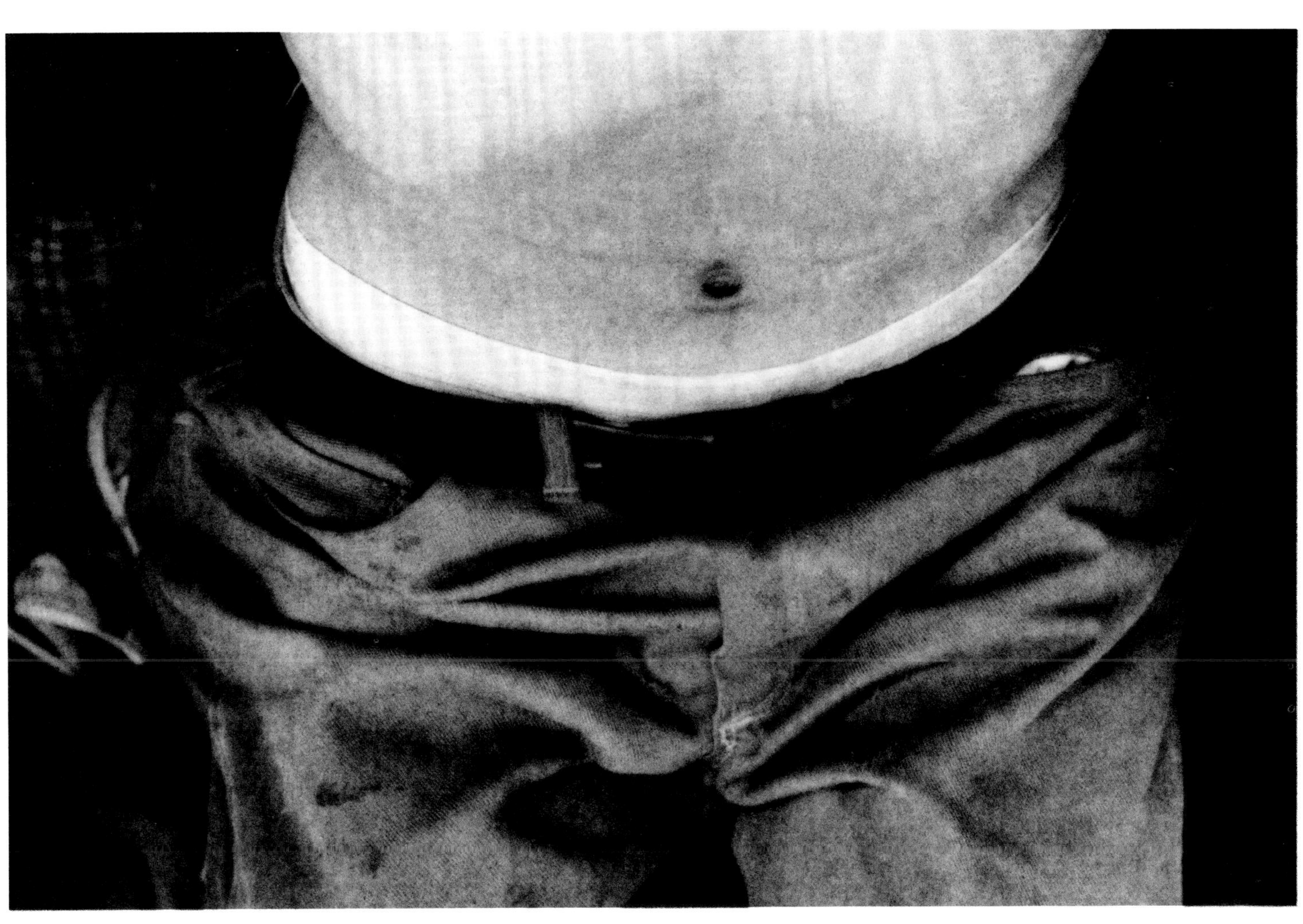

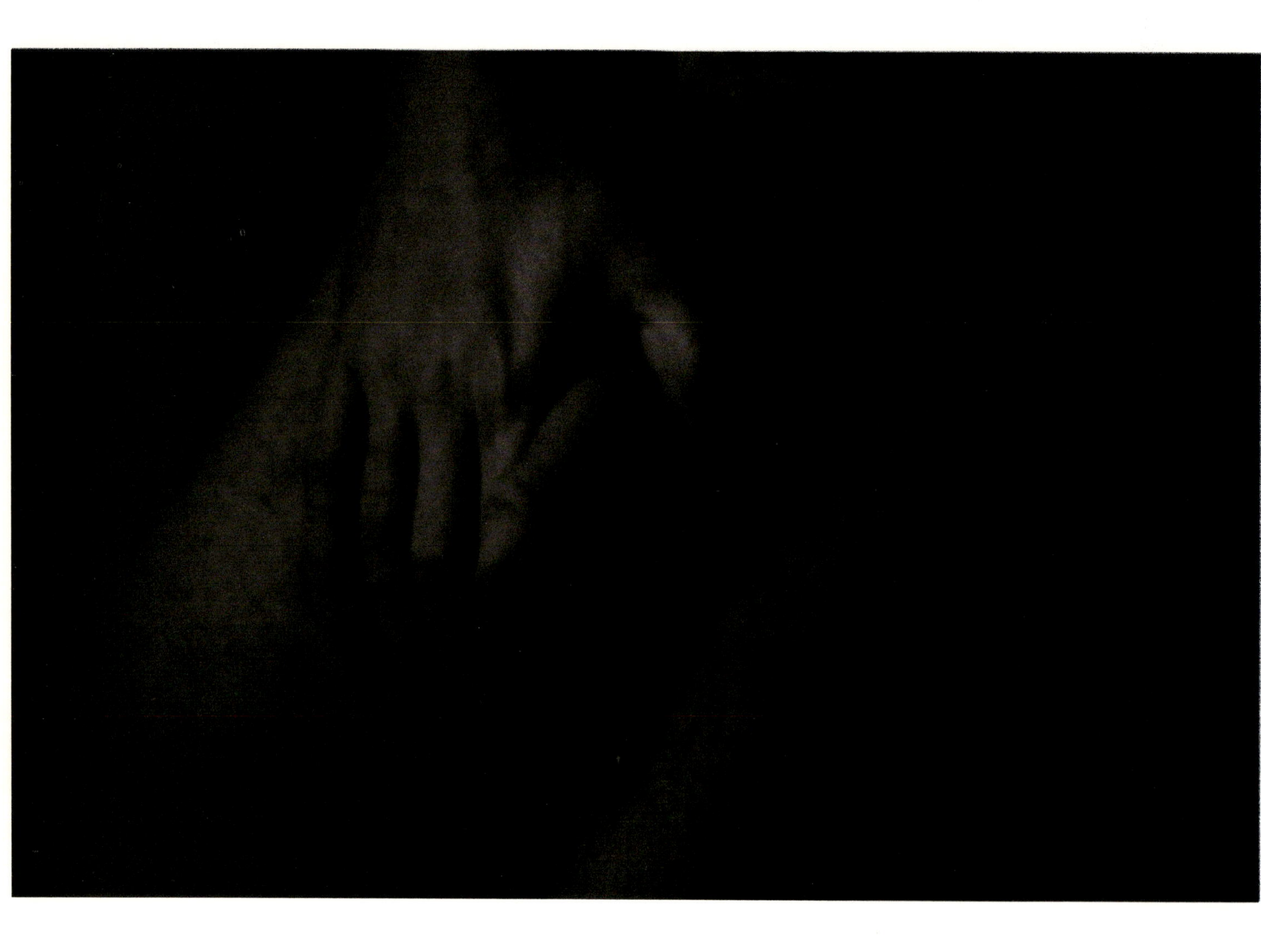

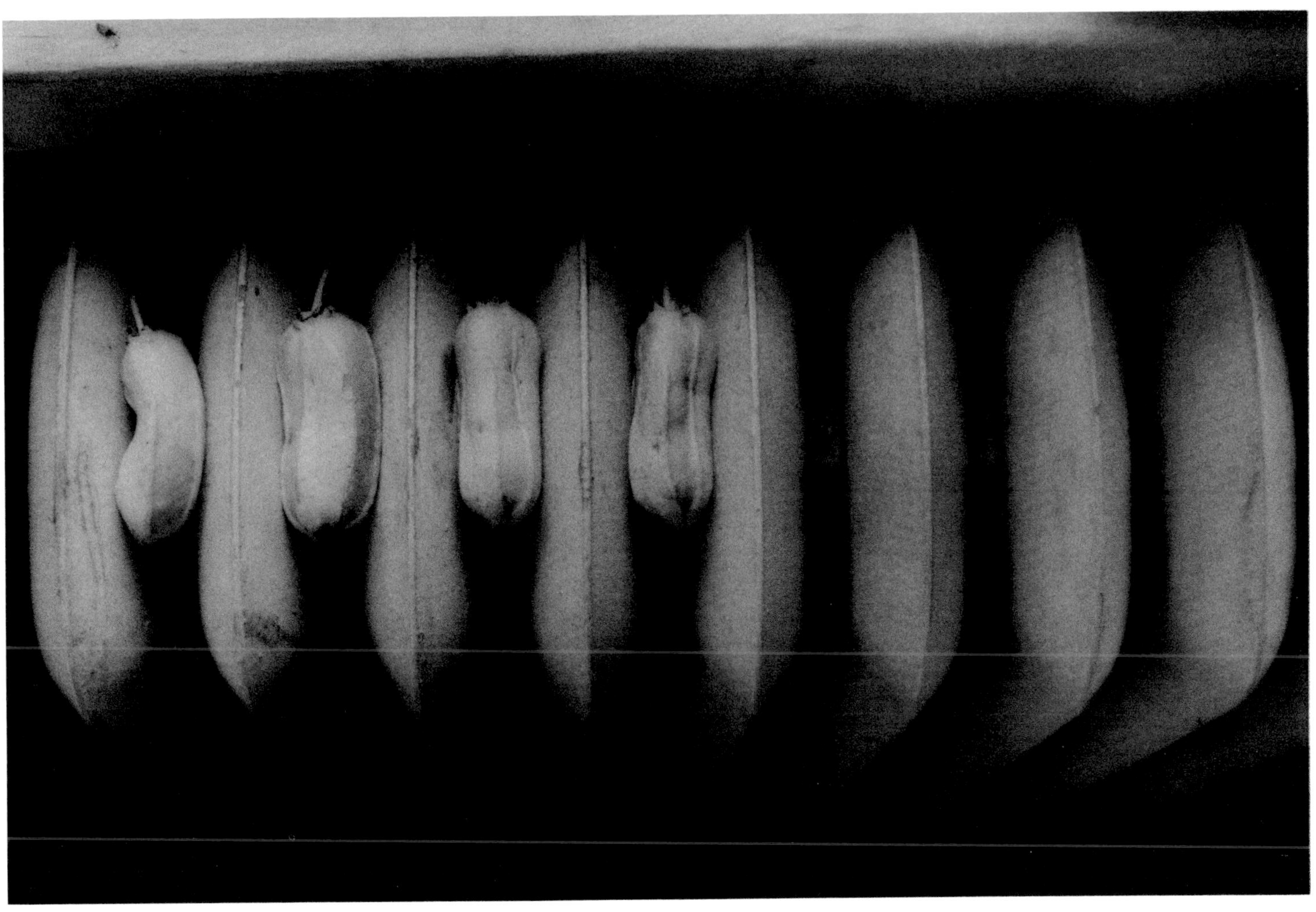

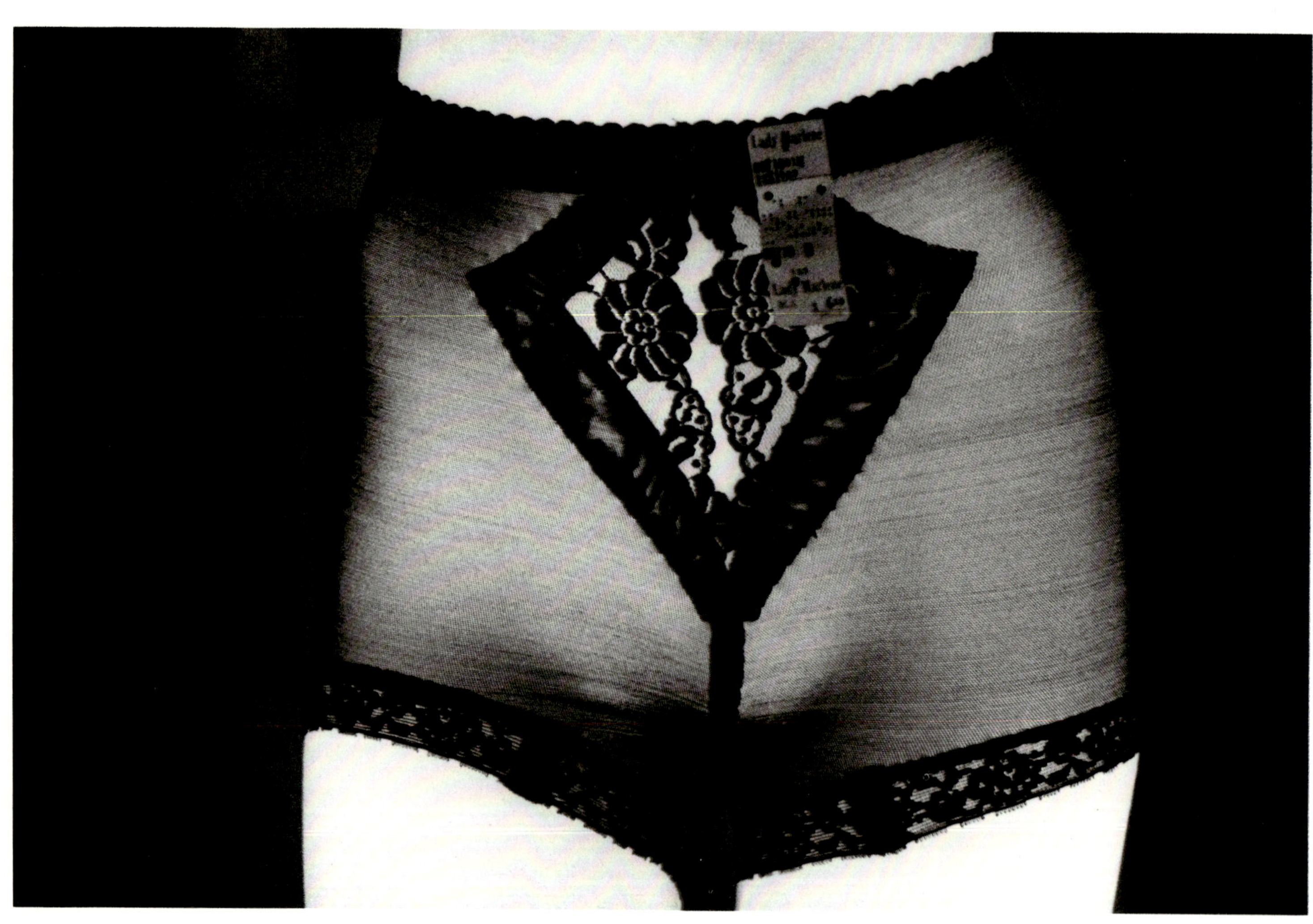

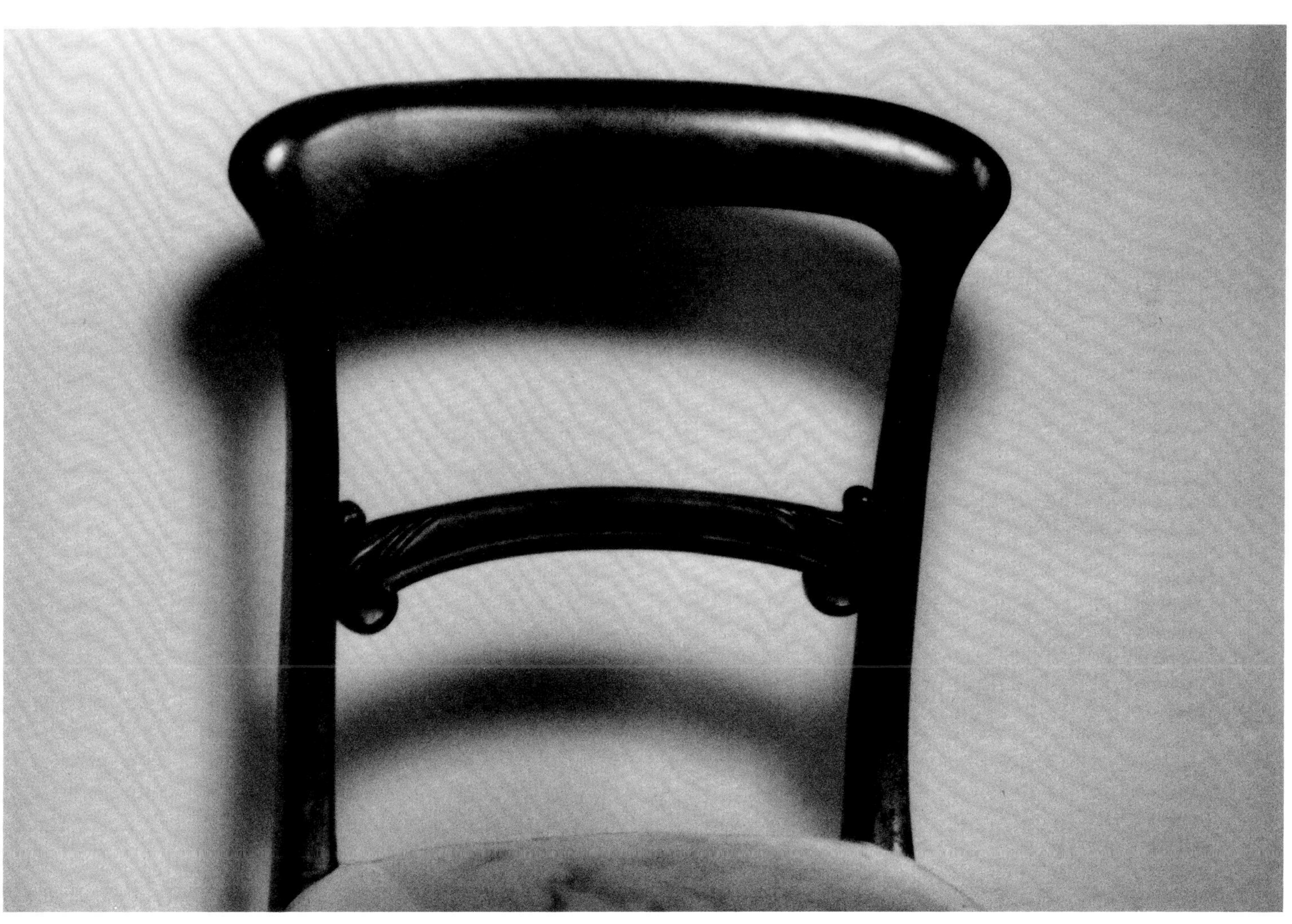

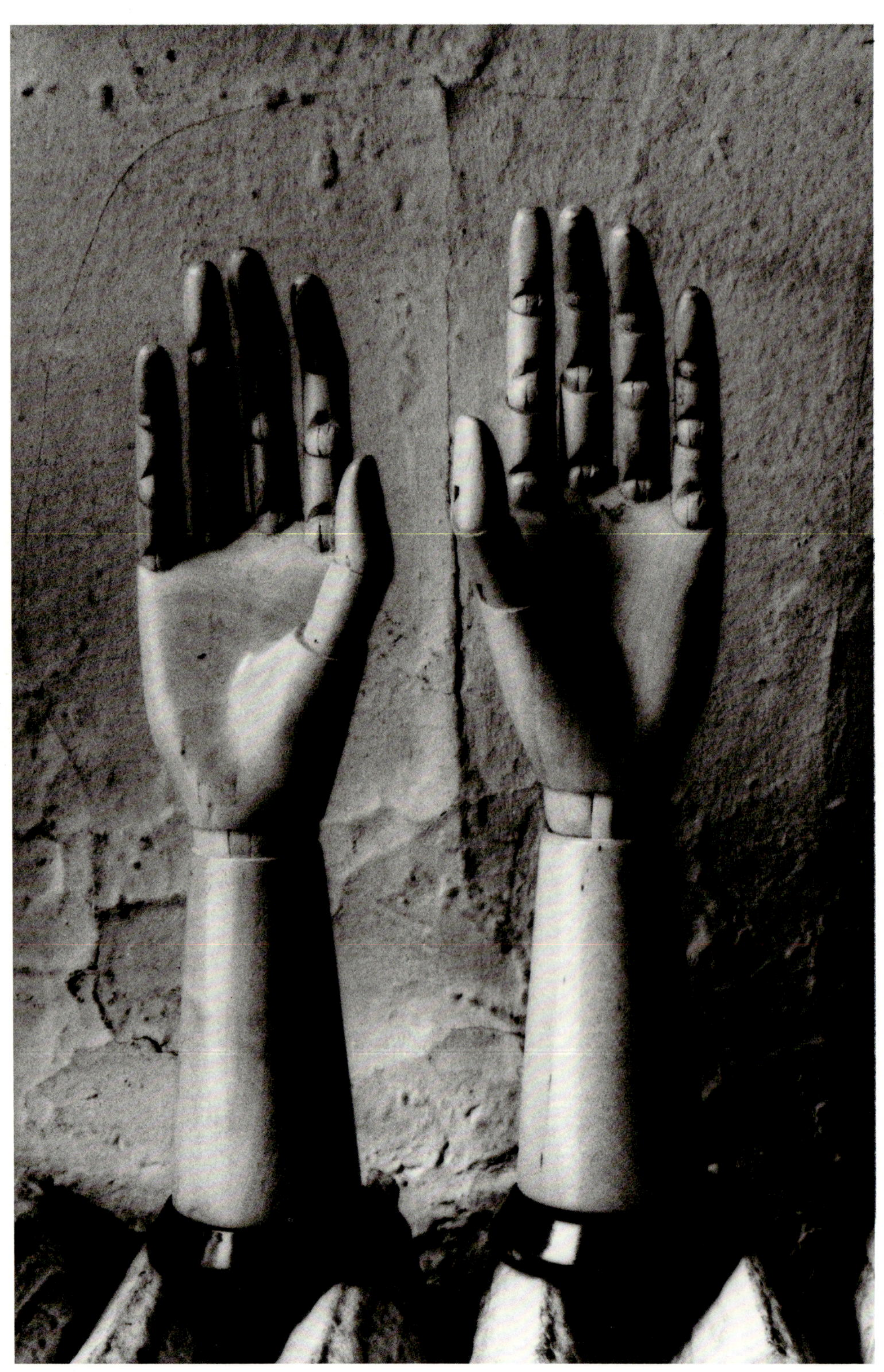

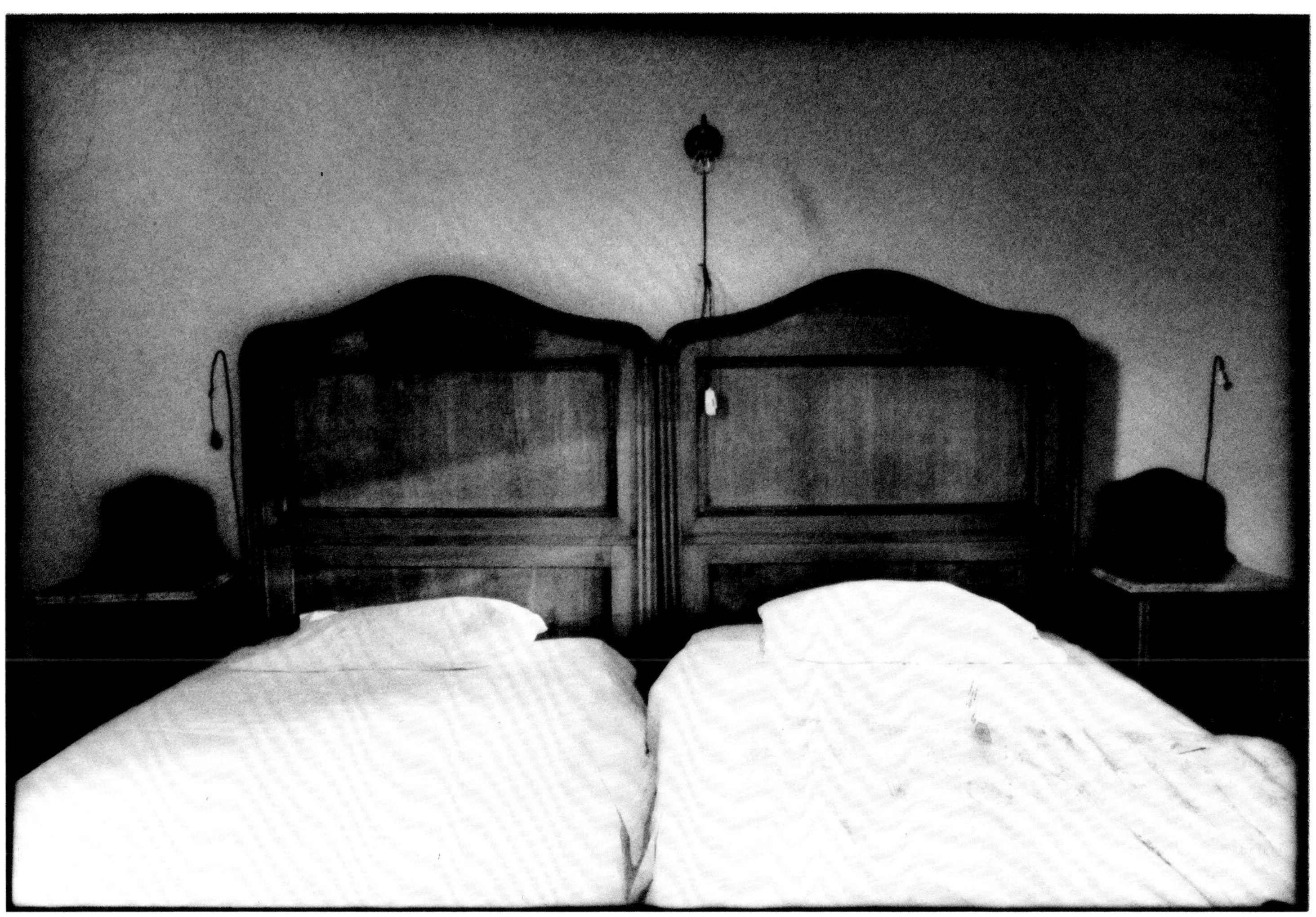

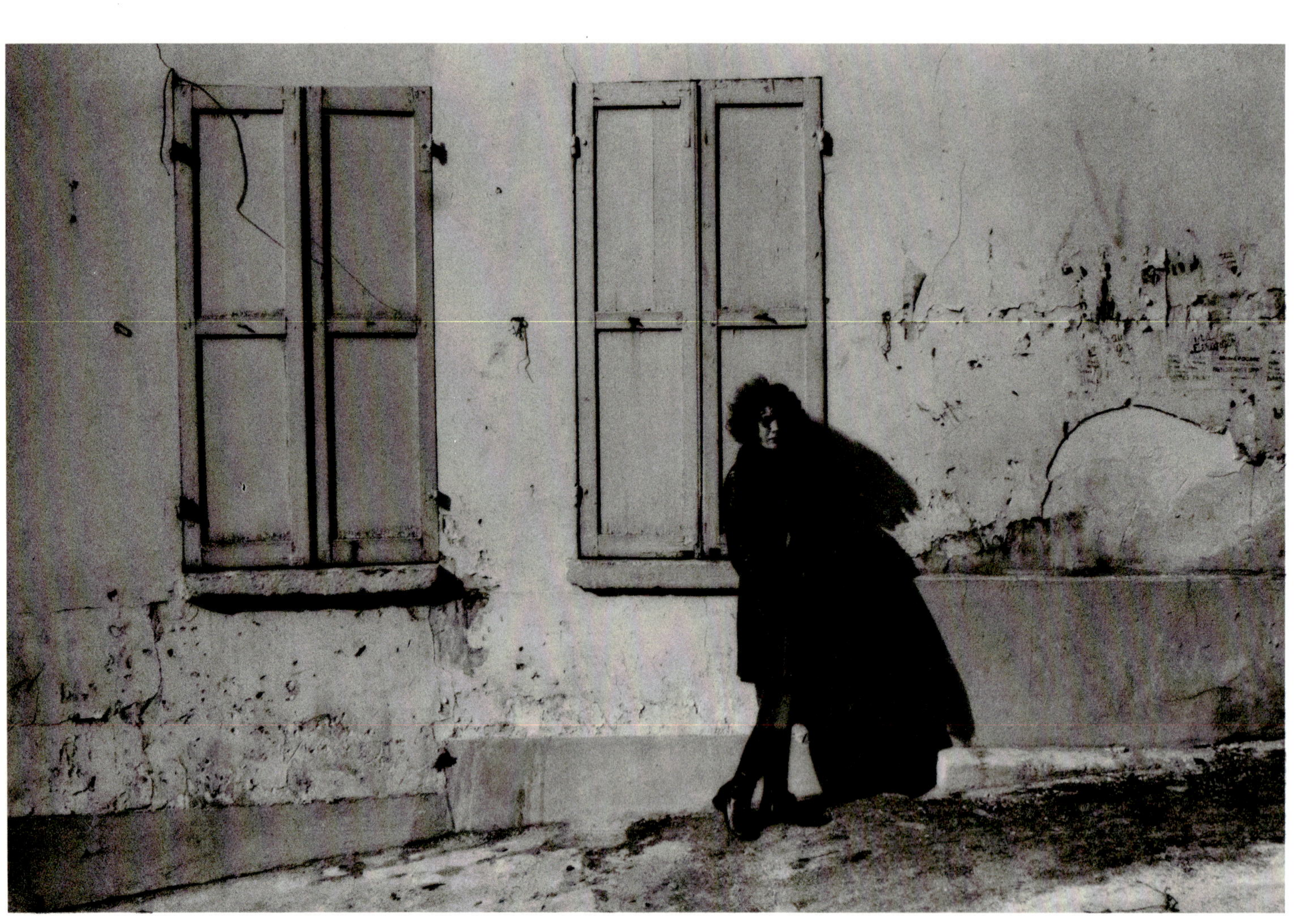

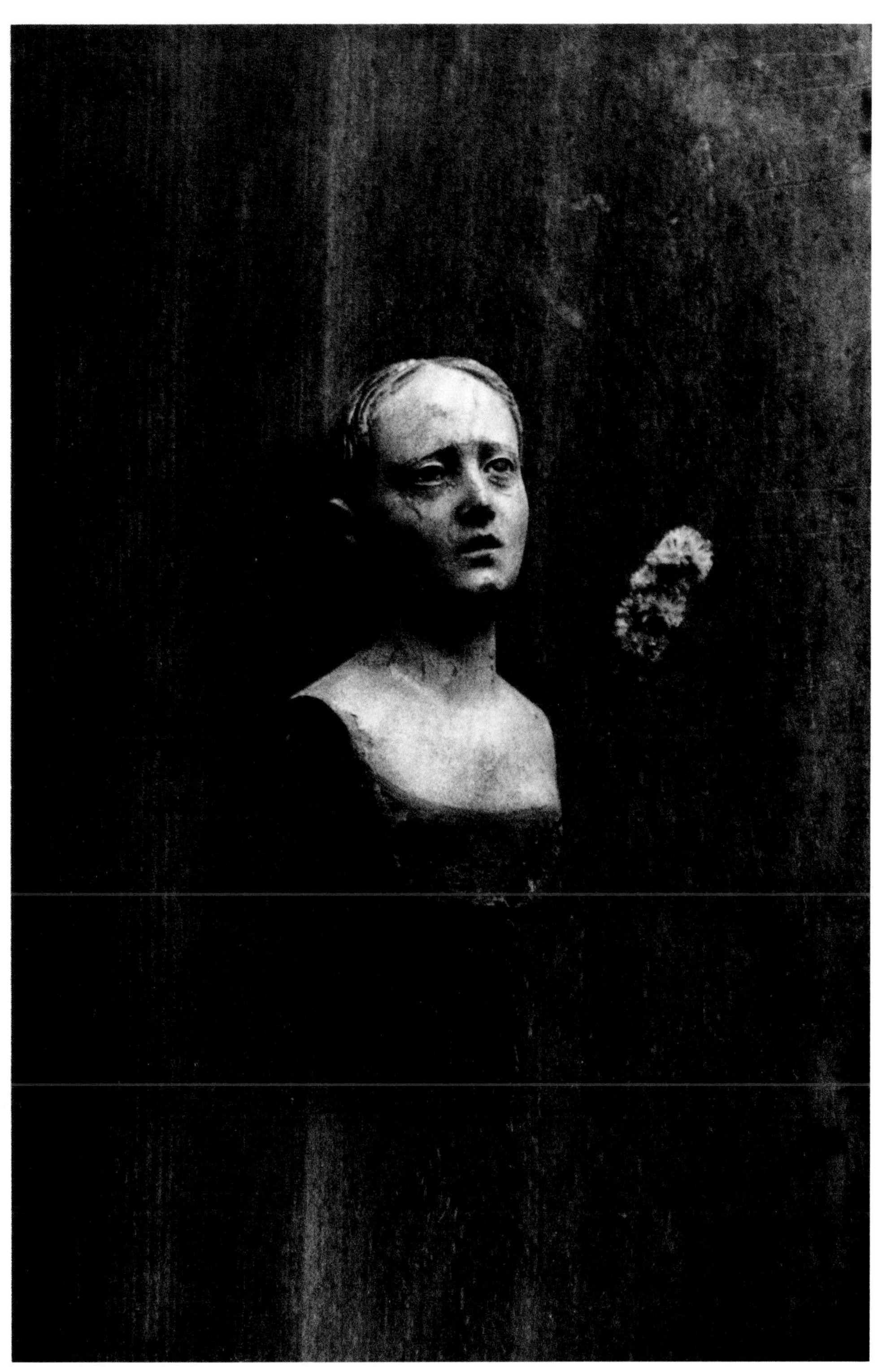

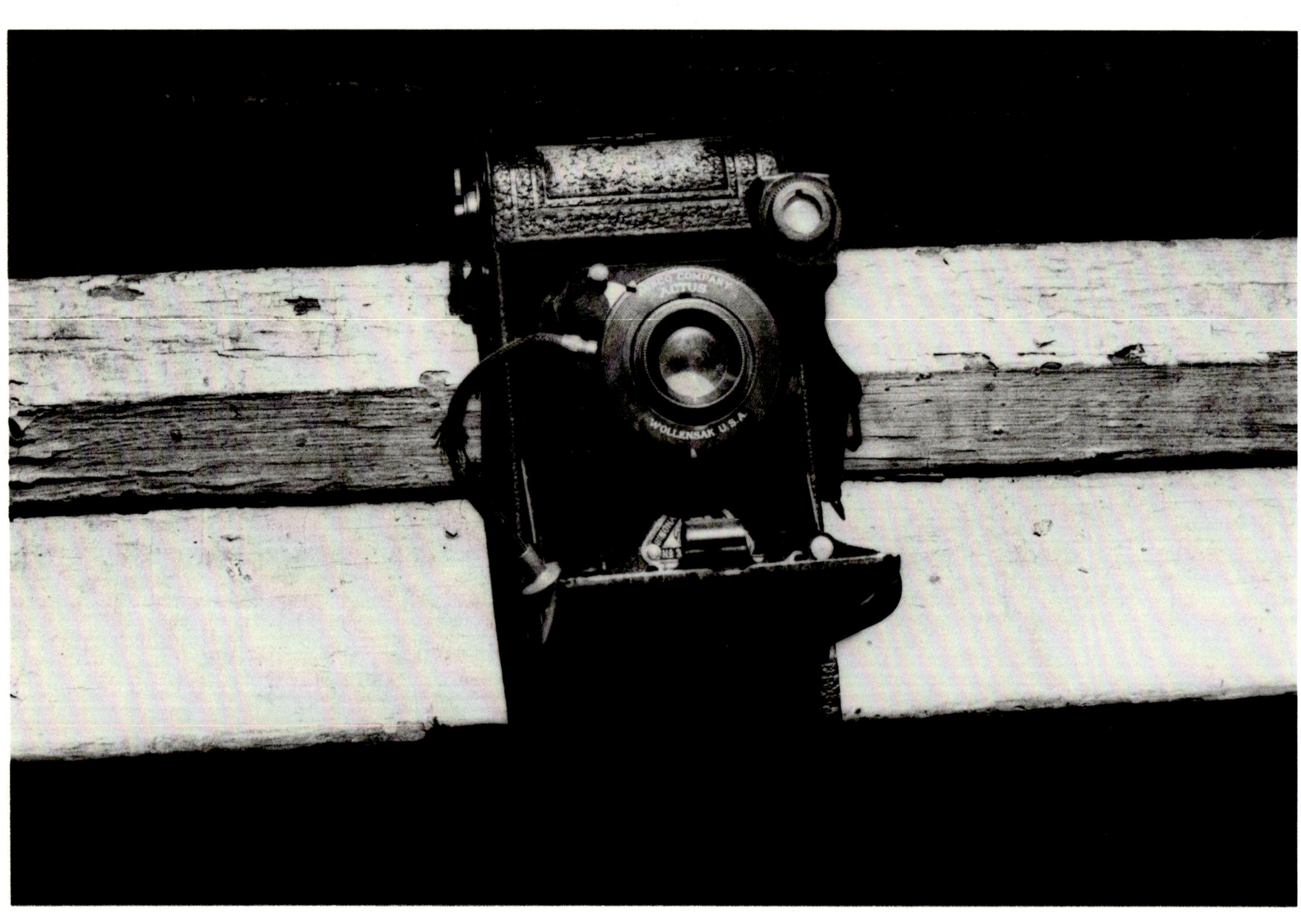
ACTUS
WOLLENSAK U.S.A.

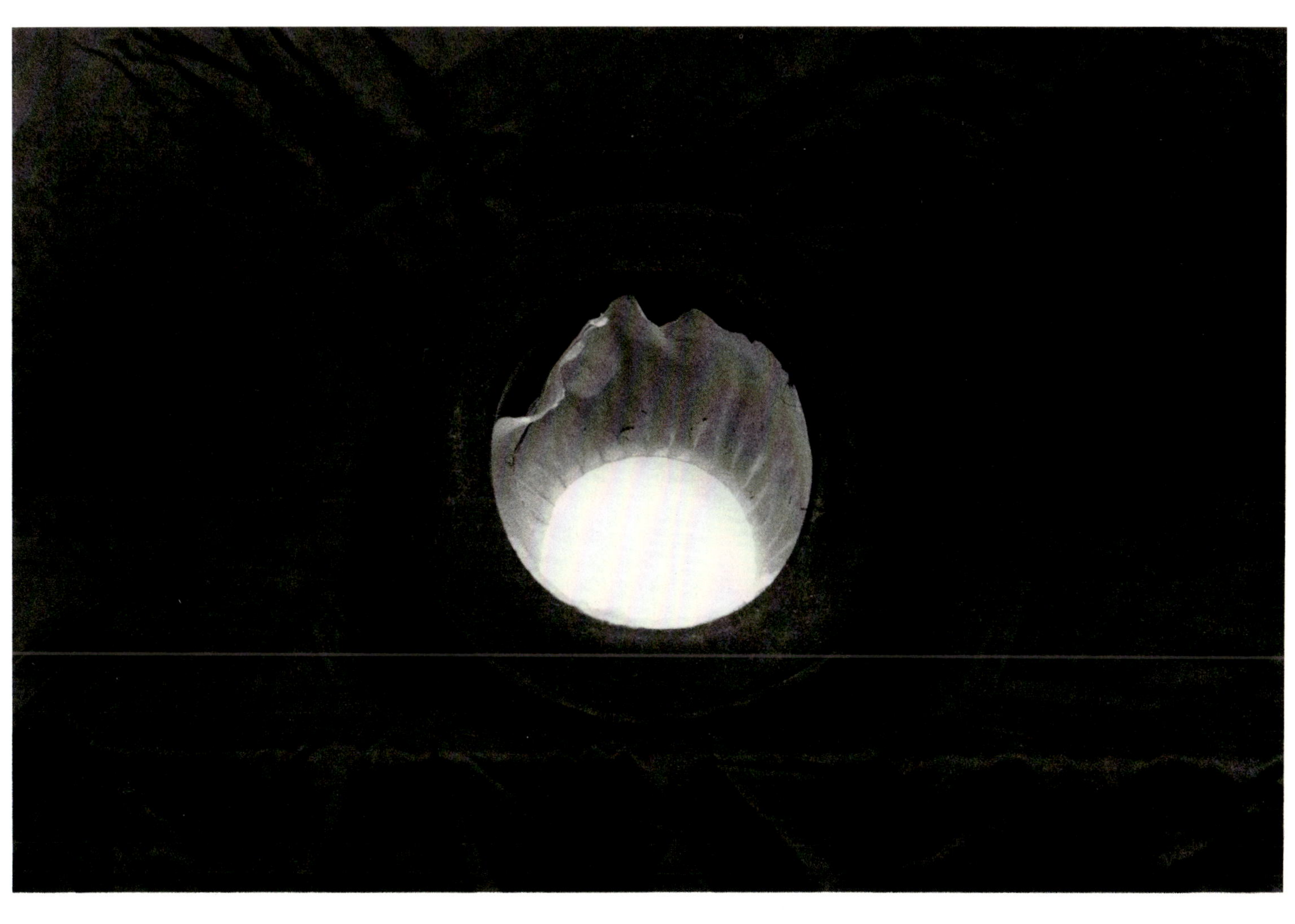